MALEVICH

SERGE FAUCHEREAU

MALEVICH

RIZZOLI
NEW YORK

First published in the United States of America in 1993 by

RIZZOLI INTERNATIONAL PUBLICATIONS, INC.
300 Park Avenue South, New York, NY 10010

© *1992 Ediciones Polígrafa, S. A.*

Translated by Alan Swan

Library of Congress Cataloging-in-Publication Data

Fauchereau, Serge.
  [Malévich. English]
  Malevich / Serge Fauchereau ; [translated by Alan Swan].
    p.   cm.
  Includes bibliographical references.
  ISBN 0-8478-1738-5
  1. Malevich, Kazimir Severinovich, 1878–1935—Criticism and
interpretation. 2. Avant-garde (Aesthetics)—Russia (Federation)—
History—20th century. 3. Suprematism in art. I. Malevich,
Kazimir Severinovich, 1878–1935.   II. Title.
N6999.M34F3813 1993   92-41509
709'.2—dc20   CIP

Color separations by Reprocolor Llovet, S. A., Barcelona
Printed and bound by La Polígrafa, S. A.
Parets del Vallès (Barcelona)
Dep. Leg. B. 40.468 - 1992 (Printed in Spain)

CONTENTS

Yuri Annenkov. *Portrait of Malevich.* 1917.

CONTENTS

Yuri Annenkov. *Portrait of Malevich.* 1917.

THE MAN AND THE BLACK SQUARE

After his death in 1935, Kasimir Malevich suffered a quarter of a century of obscurity, totally unknown to all but a small circle of followers and forgotten by history itself. Now his work occupies the prominent position it deserves in the history of twentieth-century art; indeed, so successful is his art, that in the eyes of today's young artists and art-lovers he has joined Duchamp in the Olympic gallery of the gods of art. His *Black Square* has become a symbol, a rallying-cry, a model, a point of reference and even, for those who seek artistic justification or inspiration, a pretext or an excuse. Obviously, the Russian artist cannot be held responsible for the debatable use which is made of his work. For each Jean Tinguely or Dan Flavin who have been able to develop a suggestion of his work there are as many other artists who have not understood Malevich's painterly *geste*, I was going to say heroic deed, and have only retained the anecdote, an empty form.

His deed is not legend, but founded on controlled acts, on a relationship which he himself has built up; his work is part of an epic which must be retold when one recounts the struggle of a major artist against his materials and against the received ideas of his time. But the real facts and the meaning of Malevich's work have long been considered to belong to the realm of legend. Dogged legend too often persists, since it is difficult to shake off the fascination that an accursed artist exercizes; the tragic existence of Van Gogh attracts more interest from certain sectors of the public than his work. Malevich has long been considered a martyr of art; a painter persecuted by a brutal regime, who was obliged to repudiate his work and who almost died of despair. This politicized *image d'Épinal* or popular caricature suited the context of the Cold War particularly well, but should no longer exist.

The reality is completely different. Malevich was recognized as a master. Immediately after the Russian revolution he was assigned important official functions; no other artist had as many paintings bought by the new communist regime. It is true that when the winds changed under Stalin, he came under criticism and was sometimes maligned (by other artists), but he was too influential in the art world to be seriously disturbed by these attacks. A retrospective of his work was held in the most important Soviet museum, the State Tretyakov Gallery, from 1929 to 1930 and until his death he retained his post at the Russian Museum in the laboratory where he had undertaken research on the Architektons. When he died of cancer in 1935, the funeral procession and ensuing ceremony were impressive; it was as if the crowd which had filed behind his coffin, carried on a lorry displaying *Black Square,* had guessed that with the death of this single-minded artist dedicated to his obstinately rigorous quest it had also lost a symbol of liberty; an infinitely more difficult period which would put shackles on creation and on society was to follow shortly.

The works which Malevich presented in the 1927 Berlin exhibition, carefully preserved for several decades by Hugo Häring, were at last offered to the public gaze in Holland in 1960. From then onwards, the name of Malevich returned to the lips of art historians; his writings and the first of many studies were published in the West and a little later in the Soviet Union; the Russian Museum, which had acquired Malevich's studio on his death, and the Tretyakov Gallery finally opened the doors of their reserves. It is necessary to give due credit to those who fought for the recognition of Malevich's work, in particular, Troels Andersen in Denmark, Larissa Zhadova in the Soviet Union, Camilla Gray and John Bowlt in the United States and Jean-Claude and Valentine Marcadé in France.

THE EARLY YEARS

It is significant that Kasimir Severinovich Malevich should have been born of Polish descent in Kiev in the Ukraine in 1878. After the division of Poland in the eighteenth century, many Polish families were left stranded in Russia and the Ukraine, outside the new border which had been redrawn. This explains why the artist, who had been brought up in the Polish language, whether for amusement or for reasons of diplomacy, liked to present himself as a Pole and write his name in the Roman alphabet: Kazimierz Malewicz. The artist often emphasized the importance of his upbringing in the Ukraine whenever he spoke of his influences. This explains why although Malevich belonged fundamentally to the Russian culture, he entertained privileged relationships at one or other moment of his life with Polish and Ukrainian intellectual circles.

What we know of Malevich's childhood and adolescence is told in two unfinished autobiographies.

In the more recent of these, written in 1933, he gives such vital information about his childhood that it is advisable to let him take up the story:

I grew up in the following circumstances: my father worked in sugar refineries which were generally situated in remote corners of the countryside miles from any large or small towns. The sugar-beet fields were immense and their cultivation required much labour, especially from peasants.[1]

In complete contrast to the world of the peasant in his gaily coloured costume and the fields stretching out to the horizon, the sugar mill seemed monstrous:

There, each worker followed the movements of the machines as if they were predatory animals. At the same time, they had to keep an eye on their own movements. Any false move could result in death or the loss of a limb. For the little boy I was at the time, the machines resembled carnivorous monsters.[2]

It is hardly surprising that Malevich should not share the futurist enthusiasm for the celebration of technology and machinery. He had firmly made his choice between the world of the factory worker and of the peasant:

I had always been envious of the small holder who lived, or so it seemed to me, in total liberty, surrounded by nature, who took the horses to graze, who slept under the stars and who looked after large herds of swine which he brought home in the evenings seated astride a pig, clutching its ears.[3]

Malevich owed the peasant his first contacts with drawing and painting:

The essential difference between the factory worker and the peasant is the latter's ability to draw. The former cannot draw, they cannot even decorate their own homes; they are not concerned with art. However, all peasants are. . . . The whole of the countryside is interested in art (I was not familiar with that word at the time). It would be more correct to say that they made objects which gave me great joy. It was in these objects that the secret of my attraction to the peasant lay. I excitedly watched peasants painting on walls; I helped them plaster clay on the floors of their thatched houses and decorate their stoves. The peasants knew how to paint cocks, horses and flowers devilishly well. The colours were mixed where and when they were needed, using different types of clay and blue colouring . . .[4]

The young artist would try his hand at these traditional techniques out of sheer admiration. One day, he saw a more complex painting at a fair in Kiev, he also watched three painters who had come to restore the icons in the village church. Neither parental reticence nor the frequent moves of the family from one town to another prevented the adolescent's vocation from developing and affirming itself. It was in the small town of Konotop that Malevich painted his first picture, *Moonlit Night*, which was sold at the local stationer's. He was admitted to the Kiev School of Art but shortly afterwards, in 1896, his family moved to Kursk. He had already decided to become an artist:

My painting at Kursk had developed under the influence of the "Wanderers" Shishkin and Repin, whose work I had seen in reproduction. For me, nature became the reality which I had to represent as faithfully as possible in my studies.[5]

None of these works painted from nature in the naturalist style of the Wanderers is known to have survived. Malevich was no longer a solitary painter; he exhibited alongside other amateurs like himself and, whenever he had the time, he went into the countryside to paint with his friend Lev Kvachevsky. In order to earn a living and to save sufficient money to enable him to go to Moscow, which he had learned was the home of a new kind of painting, Malevich found employment in the drawing office of the Kursk-Moscow railway. Despite the blind eye turned by some of his superiors who allowed him to draw during office hours, Malevich found the time long: "Months, whole years passed in this way, until I had saved up a little money and decided to go and live in Moscow."[6]

One can imagine Malevich's work before his move to Moscow in 1904 by cautiously examining several of the works dated 1903–4. Although most of them were in fact painted much later (Charlotte Douglas correctly

Flower Girl [1903]. Oil on canvas, 19¼×23⅛ in. (49×58.7 cm). State Russian Museum, Leningrad.

assumes them to date from the late 1920s), they are nevertheless very probably reconstructions of lost works. In fact, Malevich had always been keen that his aesthetic development be understood, and understood as he wished it to be understood, so on several occasions he repainted or returned to certain works which had been important landmarks in his earlier career.

Flower Girl, dated 1903, is an interesting example because there are at least three extant versions. The smallest seems to be a study for a larger, more detailed canvas. In the foreground a flower seller with a rather stylized and particularly small head stares at the spectator; she stands out from the pale background where a crowd is indistinctly portrayed under shadowless light. The final work has a more finished feel to it; both the flower girl and the crowd are portrayed from closer range and with greater precision; the painting has lost some of its luminosity because of the addition of shadows. A slight touch of awkwardness (the flower girl's outstretched arm bearing the bouquet of flowers is depicted in an impossible position) combines with the bold, light brushstrokes which owe infinitely more to impressionist techniques than to the Naturalism of the Wanderers; some of the elements of the composition are depicted in a precise manner (the flower girl's face and the tree to her right) while others (her basket and the crowd) are more imprecisely drawn. A few crossed brushstrokes represent the edge of a flower bed and a white form represents a woman strolling behind the girl. *Boulevard* and *On the Boulevard* (both 1903), are painted in the same manner and are set in the same urban park landscape. *Boulevard* shows a nanny pushing a pram; its simplified design and bolder colours relate it more closely to Fauvism than to Impressionism, but this seems less surprising when one considers that it was repainted towards 1928–30. *Jobless Girl* (1904), can also be included in this series of paintings.

Was it the move to Moscow and study at Fedor Rerberg's studio that led to the change in Malevich's style of painting? Whatever the reasons, from 1904 onwards there was a considerable lightening of the palette at the same time as the introduction of a hitherto unknown feeling of joy and light-heartedness in his canvases; this was partly due to the choice of subjects like *Apple Trees in Blossom, Landscape, Spring: Garden in Bloom*. A canvas like *Apple Trees in Blossom,* (dated 1904, but undoubtedly painted much later) is striking because of its luminosity and pastel tones. The lyrical qualities of such a work lie in its great liberty in relation to its realism; it is far removed from the work of the Wanderers, as the shadows are bright blue and the houses either pink or green.

From the moment of his arrival in Moscow, it would have been relatively easy for Malevich to keep abreast of developments in Russian and European art. Magazines like *World of Art, The Scales* (and later *Apollon*) prided themselves with reviews and reproductions of work of the most innovative artists; western magazines like *La Revue Blanche* and *La Plume* were avidly collected by Russian art lovers. It was precisely at this time that the two great Muscovite collectors Shchukin and Morosov began widening their interests, which had hitherto been with the Impressionists, and began acquiring neo-impressionist works. In 1904 Shchukin purchased his first Cézanne and two works by Matisse, quickly followed by his first Van Gogh in 1905; the following year, Morosov acquired a Signac. In the space of a few short years they had accumulated dozens of neo-impressionist and then fauve and cubist works. These acquisitions were in fact extremely important, since both Shchukin and Morosov gladly showed their collections to artists who were fortunate enough to examine and study authentic works of art rather than just mere reproductions. One can easily imagine that Malevich and his contemporaries Mikhail Larionov, Natalia Goncharova and Vladimir Tatlin were frequent visitors to these collections.

Despite the affluence and admirable taste of a handful of collectors, it should not be forgotten that Russia was going through a particularly troubled period of history. The extreme poverty of a huge proportion of the population and the brutality of the Tsarist regime led to the disenchantment of the most deprived classes of society who began to echo revolutionary ideas. The unsuccessful revolution of 1905, which saw Malevich manning the barricades, was repressed with great bloodshed. But despite everything, art continued to flourish; Malevich says in his autobiography:

I left for Kursk and continued to paint in the impressionist manner.... I understood that what was important in Impressionism was not to the representation of phenomena or objects in their smallest detail but pure painterly workmanship and the relationship of all my energy to the phenomena and the sole painterly quality which they contain.[7]

Portrait of a Member of the Artist's Family (dated 1904 by L. Zhadova and D. Sarabianov, but generally and more correctly considered to be from 1906), and several *Landscapes* (1906–7) of surprising pointillist technique, feature

Shroud of Christ, 1908. Gouache on cardboard, 9¼×13½ in. (23.4×34.3 cm). State Tretyakov Gallery, Moscow.

among the notable results of Malevich's study of Impressionism. Larissa Zhadova observes that *Apple Trees in Blossom* and other divisionist paintings "with their constructional use of brushwork in its own right are closer to Seurat than Signac. Yet no works by Seurat were available in Moscow then, and Malevich could therefore not have seen them."[8]

The French and Belgian Symbolists were well known in Russia; Verhaeren and Maeterlink were particularly popular. The magazine *The Scales* had secured the collaboration of poets and painters such as René Ghil and Odilon Redon, who designed the cover of the magazine in 1904. All this is relevant to Malevich, who submitted a work for show at the Blue Rose Group's exhibition. The painting in question was refused but the incident demonstrates a certain interest in Symbolism which is worthy of our attention, even though few works from this period (1907–8) remain. It has been correctly observed that Malevich was in all probability introduced to the work of Schopenhauer through essays by Valery Briusov and Andrei Biely which appeared in *The Scales* in 1904; however, as most studies on Malevich are carried out from his writings rather than from direct observation of his art, the relationship between some of Malevich's preparatory studies for a fresco, his *Shroud of Christ,* and Redon's vignettes and *culs de lampe* which also appeared in *The Scales* in 1904, has been largely ignored, yet the same haloed heads and plant motifs are present as is the figure laid out in its tomb. In *Shroud of Christ,* the symbolist imagery is given special attention; the decorative elements placed around the body of Christ are laid out symmetrically and lack depth, all the details bear the precision of a miniature. Although the imagery is characteristic of the art of the turn of the century, the work belongs to the tradition of medieval naïve painting; Malevich often expressed his admiration for icons and popular art.

FROM SYMBOLISM TO CÉZANNISM

1907 marked a turning point for Russian avant-garde painting. The Blue Rose Group had already broken away from its parent society. The exhibition entitled The Wreath held at the end of that same year went even further and brought together the future Cubo-Futurists for

the first time: Mikhail Larionov and Natalia Goncharova, the brothers David and Vladimir Burliuk, Aristarkh Lentulov, Georgy Yakulov together with L.D. Baranov and L.V. Stürzwage (who later became known as Baranoff-Rossiné and Leopold Survage in Paris). In 1907 Malevich's name appeared in a catalogue for the first time, alongside those of Larionov and Goncharova, Alexandre Chevchenko, Vasily Kandinsky and Vladimir Burliuk, at the exhibition of the Moscow Association of Artists. As a result, Malevich was able to establish contact with several of the painters, in particular the Burliuk brothers and with Larionov and his wife Goncharova, who were the leading forces of the Russian avant-garde. They were more advanced than Malevich from an aesthetic point of view, but he would not be long in joining them at the forefront of the movement.

Malevich's paintings of 1907–8 are marked by their symbolist influence. His studies for a fresco (pls. 3, 4, 5) are reminiscent of Maurice Denis's religious content and of Kuznetsov's cameo tones. We have already mentioned the intriguing aspects of *Shroud of Christ*; its conspicuous symmetry and its landscape planted with exuberant vegetation are similar to the work of the Lithuanian composer and painter Ciurlionis, although the overall finish denies this relationship, the painstaking attention paid to decorative detail and the complete absence of depth suggesting a comparison with medieval and popular art. This could also be considered true for many decorative works executed at the time, such as *Relaxing: High Society in Top Hats* (pl. 7).

Malevich would soon surpass this stage as his desire for a new form of expression was stimulated by the example of his new friends and by the discovery of western art in the collections of Shchukin and Morosov and especially in the first Golden Fleece exhibition of 1908. There were important artistic links between Russia and France; the Russians had been given their own section at the Salon d'Automne in Paris. The Golden Fleece exhibition was an opportunity for Russian and French artists to confront their works; some three hundred canvases were shown, two-thirds of which came from Paris. Larionov and Goncharova were present again, together with Kuznetsov and Saryan. The French section, which ranged from Redon and Cézanne to Rouault and Medardo Rosso, offered a fairly complete panorama of the contemporary art scene in Paris. Most of the masters of the turn of the century were present (Cézanne, Gauguin, Van Gogh, Renoir, Degas and Pissarro) alongside an important group of Nabis (Maurice Denis, Bonnard, Vuillard and Sérusier) and Pointillists (Signac, Cross, Luce, van Rysselberghe and even the young Metzinger). Of even greater importance to the public thirsting for new art was the participation of the Fauves (Matisse, Derain, Marquet and Van Dongen), whose work was completely unknown in Russia even in the form of reproductions. Certain works like Derain's views of London or Braque's views of Antwerp and la Ciotat must have particularly aroused the interest and enthusiasm of the young Russian artists; at the time Braque had not yet been tempted by the austerity of his cubist adventure. Malevich was certainly most impressed but he could not take any short cuts. At the time he was especially fascinated by the work of Cézanne which he saw in Moscow collections or in specialist Western magazines which enjoyed wide circulation in avant-garde circles. Malevich was unfailing in his admiration for Cézanne; in the last article he ever published in Russian, "An Attempt to Determine the Relation Between Colour and Form in Painting," he reaffirmed: "In the personality of Cézanne our history

of painting reaches the apogée of its development."[9] He retained principally Cézanne's liberty to handle the subject of the painting; the subject only had an interest insofar as what could be specifically derived from it pictorially: "deformation does not mean that the artist deforms the *form of the object for the sake of a new form*, but alters the form for the sake of perceiving painterly elements in the object."[10] This applies to the paintings on the theme of bathers which Malevich claims to have painted from 1908 onwards. The use of colour is measured; everything depends on the blues, greens and ochres, as in Cézanne's *Bathers*. One is above all struck by Malevich's *Bathing Women* (1908) and particularly by the three large female bodies which occupy the centre of the canvas; if their massiveness and graceless, schematic portrayal is reminiscent of Cézanne's bathers or of those shown by Rouault at the Golden Fleece exhibition, their positioning is surprising: three almost identical bodies in the same pose, rendered almost abstract by their symmetrical form and their bluish-white colour which converts them into ghostly figures. This impression is heightened by the completely featureless faces which would later also become characteristic of Giorgio de Chirico's metaphysical painting and, in a different vein, of Malevich's own work towards the end of the 1920s. This itself would tend to indicate that the *Bathing Women* in question was repainted some twenty years after the date which it bears.

Cézanne's influence would remain with Malevich for quite some time. *The Sisters* (dated 1910, but in fact a much later copy) is developed from principles close to those of *Bathing Women*. Forcefully constructed on the lines of the median of the painted rectangle, the painting thrusts forward the two pale figures of the sisters from a predominantly dark green background. They wear identical dresses and hats and hold identical sunshades in the same hand and in similar fashion, they have the same inexpressive face; the only difference between the sisters is that one is slightly taller than the other. Even when Malevich renounces the sober tones of the palette of Cézanne, the geometrical construction so dear to the French painter continues to dominate the canvas. In the works of 1910–11, where the pure colours of Fauvism made a dramatic appearance, the construction of the painting remained a primordial concern. It is based as equally on the contrast between oblique and rounded forms (*Still Life*) as on a simple upward triangular form; this is visible in the three-quarter length *Self-Portrait* which is comparable to that of Cézanne which had been acquired by Shchukin in 1908. Through Cézanne and Fauvism, Malevich drew closer to the leading edge of the avant-garde of the time; the brilliant colours and the gaily contoured shapes of the fruits and fruit bowl in *Still Life* are not far removed from Matisse's composition; the diagonal lines and the small cubes which make up the buildings of *Landscape with Red Houses* (pl. 9) should be linked to Braque and Picasso's Cézannist period which had just been abandoned. Malevich would soon be able to compare his work with that included in the new collection of western European paintings shown at the second Golden Fleece exhibition at the beginning of 1909 (Braque exhibited his *Grand Nu*, the first cubist work to be shown in Russia) and the giant international ex-

The Sisters [1910], late 1920s. Oil on canvas, 29⅞×39¾ in. (76×101 cm). State Tretyakov Gallery, Moscow.

Still Life, 1910–11. Watercolour and gouache on paper, 20⅝×20⅜ in. (52.5×51.8 cm). State Russian Museum, Leningrad.

hibition organized by Vladimir Izdebsky in the major Russian cities in 1909 and 1910. In both cases, Matisse and the Paris Fauves, as well as leading Independents like Rouault and Le Fauconnier (*Portrait of Pierre-Jean Jouve*), were shown alongside Russian artists. In the second of these exhibitions three canvases by Henri Rousseau, four

by the Italian Giacomo Balla (who had not yet become a Futurist) and a host of painters from Munich (Kandinsky, Gabriele Münter, Alexis Jawlensky and Alfred Kubin) featured among the seven hundred or so exhibited. In this way, Russia became familiar with the most recent developments in art.

NEO-PRIMITIVISM

Group exhibitions do more than serve to evaluate the progress of a generation and to affirm its aesthetic values. For an artist like Malevich with a strong will to impose himself, they will always be of crucial importance. This was the case with the Knave of Diamonds exhibition which, under the driving force of Burliuk and Larionov, opened in Moscow in December 1910. Apart from a small number of foreign artists like Le Fauconnier, Albert Gleizes and Gabriele Münter, most of the participants were Russian. Kandinsky sent four *Improvisations* from Munich; although they contained some figurative representation, they were among the most abstract paintings of the time. But other developments were taking place in the art of Larionov and Goncharova. In Goncharova's *At the Church,* a blatant lack of scale juxtaposes a standing woman and a huge face of the Virgin; Larionov provides even more obvious distortion and more aggressive colours in *Soldiers* and *Self-Portrait;* these paintings are also adorned with deliberately bold, graffiti-like inscriptions. Works of this kind are more closely related to children's art, the medieval icon and the *lubok,* a typically Russian form of folk art, than to Fauvism or Expressionism; it was not unusual to see examples of all these art forms presented side by side at avant-garde exhibitions as in the international avant-garde exhibition organized in Russia by V. Izdebsky, or by the Blaue Reiter

group in Munich. Works of this kind marked the birth of Neo-Primitivism. Malevich's radical temperament, his opposition to academic art, and above all his informal training predisposed him to this kind of art and he subscribed to it with great conviction. The fact that Malevich had grown up in the country profoundly influenced his work. Various stages of his artistic development indicate that he never forgot this influence. In his autobiography he dwells at length on the colours of the peasant world and also on the beauty of icons:

. . . the horses, the flowers and the cocks of the primitive murals and wooden sculptures. I perceived a certain relationship between peasant art and the icon: the icon is a superior form of peasant art. I discovered in this art the spiritual aspects of the *époque paysanne.* I understood the peasant through the icon. I perceived their faces not like those of saints, but like those of simple men.[11]

This discovery was crucial for an almost entirely self-taught painter like Malevich: "The study of the art of icons convinced me that it was not a question of learning anatomy or perspective, nor of restoring truth in nature, but that one must have intuition about art and artistic reality."[12] Malevich was not the only Russian artist to have held this viewpoint. Vassily Kamensky's primitivist novel *The Mud Hut* (1910) is an illustration of this, as were numerous interesting events including the exhibition of icons organized by Larionov and Goncharova in 1913 and the work of the poets and the painters of the Hylaea group, founded by the Burliuk brothers, who saw themselves as the heirs of the ancient Scythians. The difference between Malevich and the other artists is that for him this interest was not a passing fad but a fundamental element or even the foundation stone of the totality of his work. This position was shared by several of his disciples, and in particular Nikolai Suetin, who wrote: "Russian art in its principal stages has always nourished itself from the peasant environment, nature, the fields and the forest. This does not mean that it should remain so, but it does mean that this should not be forgotten on the road of artistic development."[13] It would be a gross error to infer from this interest that Malevich was a "mere uneducated peasant" as Mansurov claimed, exasperated by the diverse interpretations and influences which eager scholars had attributed to Malevich.[14] The contrary is true; he had studied popular and intellectual art, both modern and ancient, to much depth and had often discussed art with his peers. It should not however be forgotten that he was above all a painter.

From 1911, Malevich would only retain the taste for colour from his fauve manner of the two previous years. Its use for decorative effect was finished; the result was now far more primitive. *Bather* (1911) portrays a huge, red, demonic figure executing a savage dance on an indefinite but vigorously painted ground. His monstrous red feet pound the ground as if he were engaged in a "rite of spring." The move away from Fauvism seems all the greater if Matisse's giant panels *Dance* and *Music*, which had been delivered to Shchukin the previous year, are considered. There is no doubt as to the joy of Matisse's dancers; their movement springs from the ground, which is a deep green colour and contrasts with the intense blue sky; the brilliant red of the bodies, rather than giving an impression of heaviness as in Malevich's canvas, reinforces the aerial joy of the ring of dancers. Although in the same primitivist style as Malevich's paintings, Goncharova's *Peasants Dancing* and *Peasants Picking Apples* (1910) remain in the registers of Gauguin and have a more "civilized" feel to them. The same type of massive body and enormous limbs (the hands and feet are often larger than the head) render the characters of Malevich's primitivist paintings instantly recognizable: *Man with a Sack, The Gardener* (pl. 11), *The Floor Polishers, On the Boulevard, Chiropodist at the Baths, Woman with Buckets and Child* (all 1911–12) are neo-primitivist works. Malevich expressed how close he felt to Goncharova; Larissa Zhadova has also commented on this: "From a purely technical point of view, Malevich and Goncharova had much in common. Both were equally aware of what popular and ancient Russian art could give them,"[15] but it would be mistaken to say that Goncharova was the direct source of Malevich's inspiration. It is worth observing, as Marcelin Pleynet has done, that "for Goncharova the forms are an end in themselves, while for Malevich they are already no more than a means."[16] Common themes are unimportant in comparison to what differentiates them from the point of view of construction, technique and finish; Goncharova's source is Gauguin, Malevich's is Cézanne.

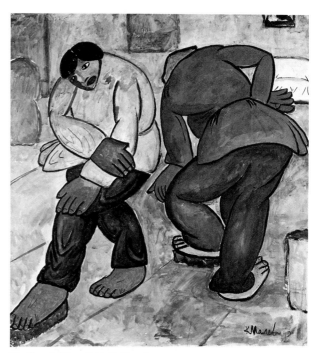

The Floor Polishers, 1911–12. Gouache on paper, 30⅝×28 in. (77.7×71 cm). Stedelijk Museum, Amsterdam.

Chiropodist at the Baths, 1911–12. Gouache on paper, 30⅝×40½ in. (77.7×103 cm). Stedelijk Museum, Amsterdam.

Malevich's own explanations of his personal interpretation of Neo-Primitivism are illuminating. He set them down in *On New Systems in Art* (1919):

We notice in art a tendency towards the primitive, towards simplifying what is seen; we call this movement primitive even when it arises in our modern world. Many people relate Gauguin to the primitive tendency, to the primeval, but this is incorrect. . . . The apparent primitivism in many contemporary artists is the tendency to reduce forms to geometrical bodies; it was Cézanne who called for and illustrated this process by reducing the forms of nature to the cone, cube and sphere.[17]

It is true that the large gouache *Chiropodist at the Baths,* similar to work executed in grisaille because of its monotonous tone, is related to Cézanne's *The Card Players,* a work which Malevich particularly admired; it has the same symmetrical effect and similar triangular construction. As for the character who occupies virtually the whole foreground of *On the Boulevard* (pl. 12), his head is a circle from which two luminous eyes shine, while the bulk of his body is a cone, like an enormous yellow sugar loaf. The painting could not be any further removed from the old-fashioned elegance of Borisov-Musatov or Leon Bakst.

In 1912 Malevich kept to themes borrowed from the peasant world. Some of his paintings feature flat, oval faces with large eyes reminiscent of masks, in particular *Peasant Women at Church* and *Woman with Buckets and Child* (pl. 13). Picasso had already painted faces which resembled stylized African masks in 1907 and 1908, in particular *Three Women* (1908) and several versions of *Farmer's Wife* (present in Shchukin's collection). In reality, Malevich's manner more probably derives from his reflection on the radical process of simplification found in peasant painting and sculpture; furthermore, his masks possess a tenderness and emotion which are absent in the work of Picasso.

In 1911 and 1912 Malevich participated in Union of Youth exhibitions, organized in St. Petersburg by Nicolas Kulbin, Mikhail Matiushin and a number of local artists; he had been invited together with several artists from Moscow, including the Burliuk brothers and a newcomer who was beginning to attract much attention, Vladimir Tatlin. Malevich met him again in Moscow at the heart of the Donkey's Tail group, which exhibited in the capital in 1912. Larionov and Goncharova had the lion's share of the exhibition, but Malevich had twenty-four canvases shown, including several of his key neo-primitivist works: *On the Boulevard* (pl. 12), *Chiropodist at the Baths, The Floor Polishers, Man with a Sack* and *The Gardener* (pl. 11). As that year the artists from the Donkey's Tail group had not participated in the Knave of Diamonds exhibition, Malevich was also absent. Alongside the Russian avant-garde artists were to be found works by the Parisian Fauves and Cubists (including five of F. Léger's canvases) and an important showing from the German Die Brücke (Kirchner, Heckel, Pechstein and Müller) and Blaue Reiter groups (Kandinsky, Marc, Macke and Münter) which Larionov, leader of the Donkey's Tail, spurned in favour of an art with deeper roots in Russia and in the East.

Woman with Buckets and Child (pl. 13) is a transitional work; the finish no longer retains the passion present in the first phase of the primitivist period. The artist plays on the contrasts between flat areas of colour and half-tones which leave the spectator uncertain as to the depth of the painting. One would be tempted to think of Gauguin because of the general tone of the painting and of the placement of the characters. The absence of one single view point and the hard edges would tend to indicate that Malevich had seen some cubist works.

CUBO-FUTURISM

In the following phase of his artistic development, Malevich further reduced forms to geometrical patterns with clearly defined edges: *Reaping Woman* (pl. 16), *Taking in the Rye* (pl. 15), *The Woodcutter* and *Morning in the Village after Snowstorm* (1912–13). In these paintings Malevich has strictly applied Cézanne's principle that everything should be reduced to geometrical forms. Malevich clearly states this in *On New Systems in Art:*

Cézanne, the prominent and conscious individual, recognised the reason for geometricisation and, with full awareness of what he was doing, showed us the cone, cube and sphere as characteristic shapes on the basis of which one should build nature, i.e. reduce the object to simple geometrical expressions.[18]

But whereas, for example, when Léger applied this principle he arrived at an almost monochromatic abstract assembly of geometrical solids, Malevich did not abandon either the figurative content of his painting or his varied use of colour. The works of this period figure among his most easily read and gaily coloured paintings: their style is close to Léger's later works. When Malevich wrote about them in *Nova Generatsiya* in 1928, he described them in terms which perfectly suit his own canvases of 1912–13. It is revealing to consider Malevich's *Taking in the Rye* and *The Woodcutter* in the light of what the artist had to say about Léger:

The construction of a body's volume is based upon truncated cones and ovoids, which, although they may be found in Cubism, have a quite different character. . . . We may say that these two pictures [*Contraste de formes* and *Seated Woman* (1913)] evoke metallic associations. . . . If we look at Leger's pictures in a black and white reproduction we will receive more of a metallic sensation since the uncoloured reproduction seems to be closer in tone to the colour aspect of the metal than its colour forms, or the forms which he has coloured himself.[19]

As the geometrical analysis of form studied by the painter develops further, to the detriment of conventions governing perspective, the works become increasingly more abstract. *Peasant Woman with Buckets: Dynamic arrangement* (1912–13, pl. 14) is an assembly of geometrical solids where the outline of the peasant woman disappears. The subject is simply a pretext; for the painter the dynamic arrangement of forms prevails. Rapid comparison with another painting of similar subject, *Woman with Buckets and Child* (pl. 13) painted several months earlier, shows how at this stage of his development Malevich had left Neo-Primitivism far behind. At the same time, his relationships with Larionov and even Burliuk, key figures of the Russian avant-garde, were beginning to show signs of strain. When in 1912 Larionov abandoned Neo-Primitivism in order to found the Rayonist movement which was connected with Futurism, he was quickly followed by Goncharova, Chevchenko, Ledentu and other artists. Malevich however did not show much interest. When the Target exhibition, which formally launched Rayonism, was held in March 1913, Malevich's works, which showed a strong cubist influence, stood out from among the Neo-

Primitives and the Rayonists present and even from the examples of folk-art exhibited: painted signs, children's art and four paintings by Niko Pirosmanashvili, the splendid Georgian equivalent of Le Douanier Rousseau. It was the last time that Malevich would take part in an exhibition organized by Larionov and Goncharova. By the end of 1913 the split had become definitive. Malevich, fully aware of his own originality, no longer wanted to be part of the group, he would begin to find his own rightful place at the forefront of the Russian avant-garde.

1913 was an eventful year for Malevich. He began to frequent the St. Petersburg Futurists who met in the house of Matiushin and Elena Guro. The poets Alexei Kruchenykh and Victor Khlebnikov and later the artist Olga Rozanova were among the most active members of this group. Together with Vladimir Mayakovsky, the Burliuk brothers and Vassily Kamensky, who were based in Moscow, they made up the core of the fertile and boisterous Russian futurist movement. Without wishing to enter into the complicated history of Russian Futurism, which was both a literary and an artistic movement, it is worth remembering that it was founded around 1910 when the anthology *A Trap for Judges* appeared; it gained public notoriety in 1912 following its violent manifesto *A Slap in the Face of Public Taste,* signed by David Burliuk, Kruchenykh, Mayakovsky and Khlebnikov ("Only we are the face of our Time. . . . The past is crowded. The Academy and Pushkin are more incomprehensible than hieroglyphics.")[20] The movement rapidly divided into rival factions which came together or split up according to the urgency of the need to combat artistic conservatism. These factions included Burliuk's Hylaea (based largely on Khlebnikov's ideas), Igor Severianin's Ego-Futurism, Larionov's Rayonism and Vadim Shershenevich's Mezzanine of Poetry (Shershenevich had translated Marinetti into Russian). Generally speaking, these groups made a point of differentiating themselves from their Italian futurist counterparts. When in 1914 F.T. Marinetti visited Russia, Larionov and Khlebnikov showed great hostility towards him. In order to deny all links with the Italian movement they preferred to call themselves *budetljane* (men of the future) or Cubo-Futurists and claim their autonomy from the European movement; for Khlebnikov "Russia [was] not an artistic province of France," and Marinetti was "an Italian vegetable" of little or no importance; at the same time, Larionov and Benedikt Livshits were intensifying their appeals to Russians to look to Asia for their origins. The Rayonist Manifesto proclaimed: "We are against the West, which is vulgarizing our forms and eastern forms, and which is bringing down the level of everything";[21] Livshits added: ". . . only when it has recognized its eastern source, only when it has acknowledged itself to be Asiatic, will Russian art enter a new phase and throw off the shameful and absurd yoke of Europe — that Europe which we have outgrown long ago."[22]

Malevich, however, although he was fully conscious of the "Asiatic" aspects of his culture, had no intention of depriving himself of what came from Europe or from anywhere else because his aim had always been to create a universal art while remaining firmly rooted in his Russian universe. This was precisely the promise he thought Cubism held, even if it came from Paris: "The new cubist body that has been built up is not opposed to life; it is a new conclusion drawn from the previous ones on the formation of the painterly movement, and has nothing national, geographic, patriotic or narrowly popular about it."[23] This divergence with Khlebnikov would never affect the excellent relations between the painter and the poet, especially as it was of hardly any interest to the rest of the group of friends Malevich had just made at the Union of Youth: Kruchenykh, Rozanova, Elena Guro and above all Matiushin, with whom understanding was mutual.

In the circumstances, Malevich's thoughts and interests clearly lay in two different and opposing directions which were nevertheless complementary for him. His personal artistic development from 1912 moved towards Cubism, an aesthetic movement which had come from Paris and for which Matiushin was both presenter and commentator; however, he was also moving towards his own alogist theory, a specifically Russian aesthetic idea closely related to the poetry of Khlebnikov and Kruchenykh and particularly their new, transrational poetic form, the *zaum.* There would be no conflict between the two tendencies.

Head of a Peasant Girl (1912–13, pl. 19) is a radical work, painted in sober blue and brown colours; conventional perspective has been abandoned and the subject is decomposed geometrically into an irregular polyhedron which is impossible to read. Malevich explained his vision of Cubism in *On New Systems in Art:* ". . . the power lay not in conveying the completeness of the thing; but on the contrary, in its pulverisation and dissolution into component elements that were essential as painterly contrasts. The thing was regarded from the intuitive aspects . . ."[24] At the same time, Malevich was working in a more dynamic style which was much closer to Futurism than to classical Cubism. In this sense, his most futurist canvas is without doubt *The Knife Grinder* (1912–13, pl. 18). Originally proposed in the catalogue of the Target exhibition as a study in the "principle of glittering," it appeared under the heading of "Cubo-Futurist Realism" in the catalogue of the third Union of Youth exhibition later that same year. Whatever the classification, the work is an explosion of gaily coloured geometrical fragments; it is decomposed by both light and movement and the figure and the narrative content can be easily read. The knife-grinder's limbs are represented in a number of positions as if inspired by Marey's chronophotography and some Italian futurist works (e.g. Balla's famous *Dynamism of a Dog on a Leash*) but, bright colours apart, the work is rather more reminiscent of Marcel Duchamp's *Nude Descending a Staircase* (1912) in that there is opposition between the dynamic and fragmented form of the knife-grinder and the simpler, static forms of the staircase and banisters. All of the works of 1913–14 are derived from Cubo-Futurism, be they dynamic like *Life in the Grand Hotel* or static like *Through Station: Kuntsevo* (pl. 21). Cubism won the day over Futurism most of the time because in Malevich's eyes it was further removed from academic representational painting and therefore gave greater scope for truly creative painting:

Creation occurs only in paintings which contain a form which borrows nothing from what has been created in nature but which derives from pictorial masses without repeating or modifying the prime forms of objects in nature. Futurism which forbade the painting of female hams or the copying of portraits has also dispensed with perspective. . . . But the efforts of

Vanity Case, 1913. Oil on wood, 19¼×10 in. (49×25.5 cm).
State Tretyakov Gallery, Moscow.

Lady at the Poster Column, 1914.
Oil and collage on canvas, 28×25⅛ in. (71×64 cm).
Stedelijk Museum, Amsterdam.

Futurism which has attempted to provide pure painterly plasticity in itself, have not been crowned with success; it could not rid itself of the figurative aspects of art in general and only managed to destroy objects in the name of dynamism.[25]

Cubism infringes on pure plasticity in works like *Desk and Room* (1913) and *The Guardsman* (1913-14). In these paintings, analytic Cubism decomposes each object in the picture into an accumulation of ordered planes, but does not allow the slightest hint of individual representation either overall or in detail. Such works belong to the realm of figurative art only in theory.

Malevich also experimented with techniques developed by Braque and Picasso and incorporated them into his own style. Thus lines were scratched into wet paint with a comb in *Through Station: Kuntsevo;* an imitation wood effect was employed in *Vanity Case* and use was made of collage. Fragments of text or photographs cut from magazines and printed documents were employed and more surprisingly, a used postage stamp and a real thermometer were glued onto the canvas of *Soldier of the First Division* (1914, pl. 27). There is much to be said about the inscriptions and signs painted or pasted onto these paintings. They can function on the same level as fragments of advertisements seen during a walk through a city: Opera, Thursday, 8, apartment, Thévenot (in Roman characters), African, etc. They are not lacking in humour either, as the large question mark in the centre of *Through Station: Kuntsevo* (pl. 21) shows, or as the hook, sole figurative element in a cubist painting which is supposed to represent a lady's vanity case (*Vanity Case*), also reveals. Sometimes the message is more complex, as in *Composition with Mona Lisa* (1914, pl. 28), which bears the inscription "partial eclipse" and where two fragments of print glued below a reproduction of the *Mona Lisa* read "apartment to let" and "Moscow"; bearing in mind that the torn reproduction of Leonardo's portrait has been crossed out in red, it becomes clear that the message directed at the old order is full of cheekiness and aggression. The defaced portrait is a visual representation of a remark which Malevich made in *From Cubism and Futurism to Suprematism: The New Painterly Realism,* "A face painted in a picture gives a pitiful parody of life, and this allusion is merely a reminder of the living."[26] What is most remarkable about these paintings and collages of 1914 is the omnipresence of perfect simple rectangles and squares of uniform colour often placed at right angles to each other. This is particularly striking in *Lady at the Poster Column* and *Soldier of the First Division,* where these parallelograms eliminate all impression of depth. If these geometrical details are taken into consideration, they diminish the effect of the brutal change produced by the appearance of the first suprematist paintings.

Malevich's development after *Head of a Peasant Girl* (1912-13, pl. 19) can be understood more clearly if one type of painting, for example the portrait, is examined. The *Portrait of Ivan Kliun* (1913, pl. 20) is still derived from the manner of 1911-12, because even though the face is decomposed into geometrical planes which render it quite abstract, the outline is still discernible and certain features of the sitter, namely his beard and the tools of his trade (a saw), are easy to identify. The overall impression of the painting is metallic and there is a certain depth of field given by the reflected light and the roundness of the planes. The later portrait *Lady in a Tram* (1913), is constructed (or deconstructed) in a more dynamic manner because the reflections of the light in the windows and the movement of the street and the tram make the surface of the painting explode, while at the same time retaining some depth. The lady's hat is drawn along the lines of force which are rendered more striking by the presence of a small realistic head acting as a repoussoir (the head, complete with bowler hat and moustache, bears a striking resemblance to Marinetti!). Overall, the canvas is reminiscent of certain street scenes of which the Italian Futurists Severini, Boccioni and Carrà were fond. The *Portrait of M.V. Matiushin* (1913) distances itself as much from analytic Cubism as it does from Futurism, yet manages to share characteristics of both movements: very advanced geometric decomposition with a real dynamic distribution of planes on the canvas. The paintings become increasingly flatter and from now on the planes are superimposed. In this instance they are more or less grouped in a square over the square canvas: they give the "sensation of planes" which David Burliuk mentions in his text "Cubism (Surface-Plane)" in *A Slap in the Face of Public Taste* (1912). The two-dimensional space of the canvas is reinforced by the presence of a small detail or two in *trompe l'œil*. Reference has already been made to the small hook in *Vanity Case*, here, a small keyhole is present; these details were obviously inherited from Braque's famous nail of 1911. As for Matiushin, the subject of the portrait, he is reduced to a few distinguishing features: his stylized hair and a very simplified keyboard which indicates his status as musician. *Soldier of the First Division* (1914, pl. 27) is no less abstract: here the distinguishing features are an ear (a feature which together with the hair was already present in Picasso's work) and a cross, symbolizing a military decoration.

It has been observed that Malevich's cubo-futurist subject matter had become urban, in complete contrast to his neo-primitive work; this was an essential feature of all futurist art which was a celebration of the metropolis, its machines and its bustling crowds. Had Malevich renounced the world of the peasant? Certainly not, since he believed that the world of the peasant was at the origin of all things and that the town was nothing but a highly concentrated form of this world: "The metropolis takes the colour energy that comes from the small centres deep in the provinces, i.e. forces which do not enter the metropolis directly, but via first of all the village, then the local and country towns."[27] It was because the metropolis had cut its roots with the provinces during this process that all was not well. Malevich, in conjunction with thinkers like Khlebnikov and the Utopian architects, became convinced several years later of the need to rethink the town.

Another interesting topic debated by the St. Petersburg avant-garde was the question of the fourth dimension. Before being adopted as the favourite battle-horse of the art historians of the time, the fourth dimension was a concept which had been derived from the research undertaken by non-Euclidian geometricians like Lobachevsky and Riemann and the physicist Minkowsky. The idea was already in the air at the beginning of the century and it would not take long to reach the centre of debates in philosophy and aesthetics. In Russia the debate was led by Piotr Ouspensky who, in *Tertium Organum* (1911), developed the work of the Englishman Charles Howard Hinton. Dreaming that the theories dealing with the fourth dimension could be applied to the arts, Matiushin became a great enthusiast of Ouspensky's ideas. He became even more convinced of their validity when he found a reference to the fourth dimension in Gleizes and Metzinger's book *Du Cubisme* (1912). He set about writing a commentary of the work by the two French artists for the *Union of Youth* magazine, translating the essential passages and supporting them with relevant quotations from *Tertium Organum*. Thus Gleizes and Metzinger's exhortation that artists should go beyond the appearance of objects had already been suggested by Ouspensky:

We see in things not only an outer aspect but an inner content. We know that this inner content constitutes an inalienable part of things, usually their *main essence*. And quite naturally we ask ourselves *where* it is and *what* it represents. We see that this inner content is not in our space. So we conceive the idea of a "higher space," possessing more dimensions than ours.... An artist must be a *clairvoyant*, he must see that which others do not see. And he must be a magician, he must possess the gift of making others see what they do not see by themselves, but what he sees.[28]

Of Matiushin's circle of friends, only Kruchenykh shared his enthusiasm. Ouspensky's "most supreme intuition" proved invaluable to him to justify his theories of transrational language, the language which went beyond the meaning of words. But painters seem to have less need to justify their work *a posteriori*; though Malevich was undoubtedly familiar with Ouspensky's ideas, he did not apply them any more than he applied the symbolism of colours. Indeed, the only reference to Ouspensky in the painter's writings is somewhat disparaging. For Malevich it was impossible to limit space; he could see five, six or a number of dimensions. He certainly did not consider the artist as a clairvoyant, even though he recognized that he could see better than others. The idea of a fourth dimension would have been at the very most a catalyst for his own ideas. Whatever the case, Malevich, Matiushin and their friends all agreed with Rozanova who stated in the same issue of the *Union of Youth* magazine as Matiushin's commentary on "Du Cubisme" that "contemporary art should not attempt to copy real objects."

Western and Russian avant-garde exhibitions, futurist publications and the ever increasing number of paintings by Picasso in Shchukin's collection were not to everybody's taste. Apart from the derisive laughter of the uninitiated general public, Cubo-Futurism also received a hostile reception from the older Symbolists and painters of the World of Art movement, in particular from Benois who launched several violent attacks and from Dimitri Merezhkovsky, who wrote in 1914: "Futurism is a scandal. It should be abandoned in silence."[29] Even in Paris, where Russian artists had sent their works for show at the 1914 Salon des Indépendants, reception was cold. Arthur Cravan in his inflammatory *Maintenant* dismissed the Cubists as painters "without talent," the Futurists as "complete nonentities" and the works of Kulbin, Exter and Malevich (*Portrait of Ivan Kliun*, pl. 20) as mere "swank." The most sympathetic reviews saw this new form of art as a break from painterly tradition. Nicolas Berdiaev, referring to Picasso, said: "Art is definitively cutting itself off from Antiquity. The process of progress in painting, which will surpass the limits of material existence, has begun."[30]

VICTORY OVER THE SUN, ALOGISM

Malevich intended to surpass Cubism and Futurism. In this respect, the circle of friends he assiduously frequented in 1913 was very stimulating for his ideas. The group included the musician and painter Matiushin, who was full of intuition; Elena Guro, the poetess who died tragically young; the audacious painter Rozanova; and the brilliant radical poets Khlebnikov and Kruchenykh. The two poets undertook to promote a form of transrational poetry which, liberated from the word, could express more than the word: the *zaum*. One of Kruchenykh's poems from *Pomada* (1913) can be transliterated as follows:

> dyr bul shchyl
> ubeshschur
> skum
> vy so bu
> r l èz

By using the *zaum* or inserting it into a text, Khlebnikov and Kruchenykh intended to transcend the meaning of common words. This idea of an abstract language which spoke without resorting to common words was of great interest to Malevich, who was eager to apply such radicalism to painting. This work was about to engage Russian art and literature in a new direction: "Alogism"; the word alone manifested the will to dispense with conventional means of expression. During the summer of 1913, spent at Uusikikko in Finland, Matiushin, Kruchenykh and Malevich published a manifesto to which they also associated the names of David Burliuk and Khlebnikov. The manifesto severely criticized "cowardice and opposition to progress" and aimed at "rushing the bulwark of artistic debility" it combined the forces of poetry and the plastic arts in order to:

1. Destroy the *clean, clear, honest and resonant Russian language,* emasculated and effaced by the language of the sacred cows of the world of criticism and literature. The Russian language is unworthy of the great *Russian people.*
2. Destroy the antiquated movement of thought based on laws of causality, toothless common sense, *symmetrical logic* and vagrancy under the blue shadows of Symbolism, and provide the new creative pro-vision of the real world of the new man.
3. Destroy the elegance, frivolousness and beauty of cheap and prostituted artists and writers who constantly issue newer and newer works in books, on canvas and on paper.[31]

Spurred on by these objectives, a number of collaborative works were written and published. Two works particularly worthy of mention are the anthology *Three,* which contained poems by Khlebnikov, Kruchenykh and Elena Guro and illustrations by Malevich, and the opera *Victory over the Sun.*

The musical work was composed during the summer of 1913; the non-sense libretto was written by Kruchenykh, while Matiushin composed the music and Malevich designed the sets and costumes. A foreword by Khlebnikov was added for the performance and subsequent publication of the piece. Although the text, published at the end of the year, has survived, all but two pages of Matiushin's score seem to have been lost. We also have a good idea of Malevich's contribution thanks to certain testimonies and the fact that the preparatory designs have been conserved. The Union of Youth patronized the two performances of the opera, at the Luna Park Theatre, St. Petersburg, on 3rd and 5th December 1913; it ran alternately with the two performances of the tragedy *Vladimir Mayakovsky,* performed by Mayakovsky himself. The two shows received more derision than applause; the opera was jeered and whistled, much to the satisfaction of Kruchenykh, who loved scandal.

The understanding between Malevich and Matiushin is hardly surprising and they worked together on many occasions; their association with Kruchenykh is more surprising as he was the most frenetic of the Russian Futurists. It is possible to see him as a precursor of the Dada spirit. But it should be borne in mind that the friendship which united the three men was based on their mutual respect. "Malevich's paintings," wrote Kruchenykh in *Three,* "are creations which resemble purely Russian intransigence."

Victory over the Sun is a vast lyrical rodomontade and the details and overall action of the plot are extremely difficult to grasp. A host of futurist and reactionary characters taken from all environments and periods of history file on and off and confront each other around the sun, which is the emblem of old-world conservatism. The element of humour present in the bewildering speeches of the characters should not be underestimated. Malevich's sets and costumes are no less surprising. So much attention has been paid to the suprematist simplicity of most of the backcloths, based on the geometry of the square, and to the white walls and black floor that the interesting contrast between their simplicity and the complexity of the costumes has been largely neglected. The costumes were extremely varied, their colours and geometric shapes (cloth, and cardboard cones and cylinders) as well as the geometric appendages which the actors wore leave no doubt as to their futurist origin. Livshits declared that:

[the] figures were cut up by the blades of lights and were deprived alternately of hands, legs, head, etc. because, for Malevich, they were merely geometric bodies subject not only to disintegration into their component parts, but also to total dissolution in painterly space.... This was a zaum of painting.[32]

Despite its disjointed plot and the fact that the opera seems to anticipate Dada by dint of its lack of apparent logic, *Victory over the Sun* is a totally futurist work in subject. The attack on the sun takes up the ongoing debate about light in which Marinetti, Balla, Severini and other Futurists had embarked. Strangely, the sun is a symbol of very down-to-earth rationality for Malevich; in *On New Systems in Art* the tenth resolution in art is "To relate the sun as a bonfire of illumination to the system of our earth of flesh and bones."[33] The fascination for aviation is one domain where the Russian Futurists were a step ahead of the Italians. The month before *Victory over the Sun* was performed, Vassily Kamensky gave a lecture entitled "Aeroplanes and Futurist Poetry" in

Victory over the Sun, costume design: the Enemy. Pencil, ink and watercolour on paper, 10⅝×8⅜ in. (27.1×21.3 cm). Theatrical Museum, Leningrad.

Victory over the Sun, costume design: the Reciter. Charcoal, ink and watercolour on paper, 10¼×8⅜ in. (27.2×21.4 cm). Theatrical Museum, Leningrad.

Victory over the Sun, costume design: the Malevolent One (A Certain Guy with Bad Intentions). Pencil, ink and watercolour on paper, 10¾×8¼ in. (27.3×21.3 cm). Theatrical Museum, Leningrad.

Moscow. He knew what he was talking about; two months previously he had abandoned flying after his plane had crashed at an aerobatics meeting in Poland. In the eyes of his friends, this flying accident was to become as legendary as Marinetti's automobile accident to the Italian Futurists. The aviator emerged a hero from the failure of his Promethean adventure. In the last scene of *Victory over the Sun* a plane crashes onto the stage and the unscathed pilot says laughing heartily: "Ha ha ha, I am alive. I am alive only the wings are a little shabby and my shoe!"

The closing lines of the opera prophetically express a bragging optimism typical of all Futurisms:

> Everything is good that
> has a good beginning
> the world will die
> but for us there is no end![34]

Victory over the Sun also marked a beginning for Malevich. When Matiushin was attempting to publish the libretto of the opera, Malevich persistently pleaded with him to include the drawing of the backcloth from the victory scene because "this drawing will have great significance for painting. What has been done unconsciously is about to bear extraordinary fruits."[35] Malevich had the intuition that this backcloth with the large black and white square was going to contribute to the founding of Suprematism. It was for this reason that Malevich always gave the date for the foundation of Suprematism as 1913, although strictly speaking the first suprematist paintings date from 1915. Malevich had not quite arrived at Suprematism but he had entered a specific phase of Russian Cubo-Futurism, Alogism, and *Victory over the Sun* was one of the first (and finest) examples.

While working on his essay *On New Systems in Art* in 1919, Malevich claimed that Alogism was one of the direct consequences of Cubism: "Thus Cézanne laid the outstanding and significant foundations of the cubist trend which flourished in France with Braque, Picasso, Léger, Metzinger and Gleizes, and which emerged in Russia with the new bias towards Alogism."[36] Although largely derived from the cubist system, certain works like *Composition with Mona Lisa* (pl. 28) contain juxtapositions of objects and signs which are unusual to say the least. This is also the case with *Cow and Violin* (1913, pl. 22), a work which is visibly too disconcerting to be properly classed as cubo-futurist. In this painting Malevich superimposed a small but realistic cow on a stylized but easily recognizable violin which is pushed forward from the geometrical background. The only two recognizable figurative objects clash violently for several reasons; they belong to two different realms of reality which rarely meet, they are presented together in a situation which totally ignores both perspective and scale and they are depicted in two antithetical manners; the cow is a typical subject for rural realist painters whereas the violin, object of urban culture, is a favourite motif found in cubist still-lifes. It is true that in *Du Cubisme* Gleizes and Metzinger state that "painting has the power to transform what we consider to be tiny into something enormous, and what we believe to be important into something insignificant: it can change quantity into quality." Matiushin emphasized this idea in his review of 1913 and Malevich took it further when he stated that "the scale of each form is arbitrary."[37] In this specific example, it is not only scale which is called into question and we find ourselves closer to analogy as defined by Marinetti in his *Technical Manifesto of Futurist Literature* (1912): "Analogy is nothing but the immense love which unites distant things which are apparently different and hostile. It is through extremely vast analogies that the orchestral style, which is at the same time polychromatic, polyphonic and polymorphous, can embrace the life of matter," or even closer to the "very high degree of immediate absurdity" which the *Surrealist Manifesto* required of its images. Malevich added his own comments on the reverse of *Cow and Violin:* "Alogical collusion of two forms, the violin and the cow, illustrates the moment of struggle between logic, natural order, bourgeois sense and prejudice." One cannot but delight at the delicious challenge to common sense that such illogical confrontations provide (akin to

Victory over Sun, Stage Design, Act 1, Scene 3.
Pencil on paper, 7×8¼ in. (17.7×22.2 cm).
Theatrical Museum, Leningrad.

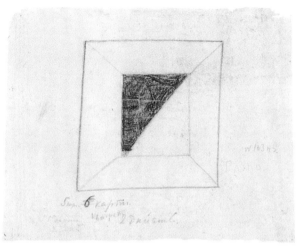

Victory over the Sun, Stage Design, Act 2, Scene 5.
Pencil on paper, 8¼×10⅝ in. (21×27 cm).
Theatrical Museum, Leningrad.

the famous nursery rhyme "Hey diddle diddle, the cat and the fiddle, the cow jumped over the moon.") In 1913, several of Malevich's letters to Matiushin speak of "rejecting reason" or "surpassing reason."

An Englishman in Moscow (1914, pl. 29), is the most famous of Malevich's alogist paintings. It shows a man surrounded and partly concealed by a completely inconsequential series of objects: a large fish, a candle and holder, a red arrow, a tiny church, a ladder, a wooden spoon and several sharp instruments — a sabre, a saw, a pair of scissors and a row of bayonets. Various clues indicate that the subject is a Futurist, particularly the top hat and the red wooden spoon which Russian Futurists wore as a sign of provocation; the title could easily be a reference to the aggressive Kruchenykh who, according to his friends, dressed like an Englishman. A further private joke could be the words "Riding Club" which are supposed to represent the quintessence of an Englishman; the words "partial" and "eclipse," already encountered in *Composition with Mona Lisa*, also appear on the canvas. The painting probably refers to the ongoing futurist debate about the sun and light; the dark outline of the head and shoulders of the librettist of *Victory over the Sun* partially covers the sun and a few rays of sunlight are seen emerging from behind his head in the top left hand corner of the painting. He can easily be imagined singing the following words from the opera: "The sun hid / darkness fell / we will all take knives..."

The Aviator (1914, pl. 30), alogist portrait of another futurist friend, offers an equally strange effect: Kamenski, the subject of the portrait, is wearing a top hat adorned not with a spoon but with a large fork. He is holding the ace of clubs which may be taken to represent the love of gambling, the love of risk or even the sign for money among fortune-tellers. It could also refer back to the club-shaped head of one the strongmen in *Victory over the Sun*. Although it is difficult to identify an aircraft or any other object in the mass of shapes which surround the figure, it is possible to identify a large fish and a saw, as in *An Englishman in Moscow* (pl. 29). The word "Pharmacy" can be taken to be a reference to Kamenski's aviation

accident while performing stunts in his plane; additionally, the last syllable of the Russian word "Apteka," which in this instance is separated from the rest of the word, is also the first syllable of the flying poet's name. Obviously, apart from a small circle of friends familiar with the circumstances, all other spectators would have seen nothing but an accumulation of absurdities defying all the precepts of common sense. Even when he was no longer exploiting the potentially provocative aspect of his alogist paintings, Malevich would not abandon this attitude which aimed to transcend reason. In his "Easter Greetings" of April 1915 he wrote: "Reason is a gaoler's chain for the artist, this is why I would like all artists to lose their reason." Then, in 1916, in a pamphlet entitled "Secret Vices of the Academicians," also containing texts by Kruchenykh and Kliun, he published the following phrases which were symptomatic of a whole period:

A work of the highest art is written in the absence of reason.
A fragment from such a work:
"I have just eaten calves' feet."
It is surprisingly difficult to adjust oneself to happiness having travelled the length and breadth of Siberia.
I always envy the telegraph pole. A chemist's shop.
Of course many people will think that this is absurd, but in vain. One has only to light two matches and set up the wash-stand.[38]

Such declarations clearly anticipate the Dada manifestoes and also indicate a frame of mind specific to the Dadaists; it was not possible however that Malevich could have been familiar with Duchamp's ready-made entitled *Pharmacy* (1914), or indeed with his future work consisting of an urinal, *Fountain* (1917), nor the collage of matches, hair clips and coins of Francis Picabia's much later work *La femme aux allumettes* (1924–25). Despite his provocative behaviour, Malevich would never choose to join the Dada movement. During 1914, he painted in two distinct styles: cubist and cubo-futurist works like *Portrait of Matiushin*, and alogist works like *An Englishman in Moscow*. In Malevich's eyes, Cubism and, to a lesser degree, Futurism were still "an attempt by reason, as the protector of logic."[39] Alogism on the other hand upset reason but did not satisfy the artist completely from a formal point of view. However, the combination of both of the above forms of aesthetic thought would allow him to find another solution. Simple, two-dimensional figures which were becoming omnipresent in cubo-futurist compositions would grow and take possession of the whole canvas without making any reference to models taken from the outside world which alogical will had finally liberated. Suprematism was born.

SUPREMATISM AND THE BLACK QUADRANGLE

In retrospect it is easy to look back and to say how Suprematism was inevitable. It is clear however that the square on the backcloth in *Victory over the Sun* would haunt Malevich's subsequent work. Flat geometrical planes, already present in *Cow and Violin* (pl. 22) in 1913, were to invade the paintings of the following year, e.g. *Soldier of the First Division* (pl. 27) and *Composition with Mona Lisa* (pl. 28). The blue square of the former and the black rectangle of the latter have an overpowering presence on the canvas. In *Composition with Mona Lisa* the inscriptions "partial eclipse" or "apartment to let," which ironically refer to the Mona Lisa crossed out in red and the space she occupies, are less surprising than the geometrical figures around her; these shapes seem to want to have a life of their own on the canvas over and above all other consideration; if it were not for the collage and the black lines, the painting would be very close to suprematist abstraction.

Malevich wrote: "The twentieth century is marked by sharp opposition on the part of painters and poets to objectivity. The former arrived at non-objectivity, the latter at 'zaumnost' (against both of which the Objectivists and politicians have again raised their banner)."[40] As Malevich always connected the work of Suprematists and of his friends the *zaumniks*, it would be interesting to see how Kruchenykh justifies this imaginary language in his *Declaration of the Word as Such:*

Thought and speech cannot catch up with the emotional experience of someone inspired; therefore, the artist is free to express himself not only in common language (concepts), but also in a private one (a creator is individual), as well as in a language that does not have a definite meaning (is not frozen), that is *transrational*. A common language is binding; a free one allows more complete expression (e.g. ho osnez Kayd, etc.).[41]

Khlebnikov distances himself somewhat from this definition in that he sees the zaum as the prerogative of all, it is a universal language and not an individual creation. In the same way that words are unburdened of their common form and meaning in the zaum, so too suprematist painting will be liberated from all form originating in the ordinary world; the new language of this movement will derive from elementary figures and will not be related to anything known.

Malevich participated in public recitals of transrational poetry; for their part, the poets concerned listened to his ideas and were moved by his paintings. Khlebnikov was thinking of Malevich's research when he wrote his speech to the Artists of the World: "The artist's task would be to provide a special sign for each type of space. Each sign must be simple and clearly distinguishable from all the rest."[42] Many of the Russian futurist painters and poets seemed to be heading towards the "zero level." This can be seen by considering *Death to Art* (1913), a booklet of poems by the ego-futurist poet Vasilisk Gnedov prefaced by Kazanski Ignatiev. The preface prophesied the imminent extinction of the word and claimed that highly organized intuition would allow true transrational communication to take place. Vladimir Markov describes the poems in the following terms:

Of fifteen poems by Gnedov, nine are one-line poems, most of them consisting of neologisms. One poem (no. 6) uses seemingly meaningless syllables; another (no. 9) simply repeats a word (or name?) three times; two poems, though bearing neologistic titles, use known Russian words. Of the rest, two consist of one neologistic word each, and two of just one letter each. Finally, page eight, which is also the back cover of the book, has only the title of poem number 15, *Poema Konsta* "Poem of the End."[43]

In his foreword Ignatiev describes how Gnedov performed this last poem: "He read [it] with a rhythmic movement. The hand was drawing a line: from left to right and vice versa (the second one canceled the first, as plus and minus result in minus). 'Poem of the End' is actually 'Poem of Nothing,' a zero, as it is drawn graphically."[44] Does this example, which gives a good idea of the intellectual climate shortly before the Revolution of 1917, mark a blind alley or a new start? Ignatiev committed suicide the following year, and Gnedov, cruelly deprived of his master, disappeared not long after the publication of the booklet. But zero is also the point from where everything becomes possible anew (in the West the nihilism of Dada was followed by the birth of Surrealism). For a painter like Malevich, with such a thoroughly positive spirit, a return to zero was not a nihilist gesture but a return to the humblest of origins where he found himself liberated from the shackles of convention. His position was in many ways similar to Kupka's, who after a different artistic development in the West began writing *Creation in the Plastic Arts.*

Yet Malevich did not seem to have fully made the transition to non-figurative art by the beginning of 1915. At the futurist Tramway V exhibition, where he participated alongside Rozanova, Popova, Exter, Udaltsova, Puni, Tatlin, Kliun and Morgunov, he exhibited only cubo-futurist and alogist works. It was not until the summer that his research, carried out in the secrecy of his studio, bore fruit and he produced his first suprematist works. He worked without interruption and in December he exhibited thirty-six new non-figurative works at 0.10, the last futurist painting exhibition in St. Petersburg; these included *Black Square*, which raised a general outcry. Cubo-Futurism and its offshoots had now been surpassed, which explains why 0.10 was the last exhibition: "I have been transfigured in the zero of forms and have emerged beyond 0.1. Considering that Cubo-Futurism has fulfilled its objectives, I now move to Suprematism, to new painterly realism, to non-figurative creation."[45] The surprise which Malevich had counted on creating was somewhat lessened by the fact that several of his close friends, including Kliun, Popova, Rozanova, Puni and Exter, had followed him in his new direction as soon as they had learned about it. A short manifesto was also released. To mark the date and to show his pre-eminence in the art world, Malevich also published *From Cubism to Suprematism: New Painterly Realism*, a seminal work which was revised twice the following year. He further expanded his theories on Suprematism in 1919 and 1920 in *On New Systems in Art, From Cézanne to Suprematism* and in the illustrated book *Suprematism: 34 Drawings.*

Malevich's writings on art are often difficult to follow, the arguments are seldom developed conventionally and jump back and forth only to express the same idea differently. Certain art historians who are otherwise well disposed to him have lost patience with his writings. Dora Vallier wrote:

His work as an artist, which preceded his work as a theorist, followed a structured development, but his writings once they reach a certain length become so dense that it seems difficult to imagine that they were ever fully revised or corrected, probably due to lack of patience. It is as if Malevich shied away from any definitive version of his writings. His lively thought which is in constant movement is dispersed all over his work and he continually returns to ideas as if to inspect them more closely.[46]

Nevertheless, to understand how Malevich evolved from Cubo-Futurism and Alogism to the most extreme of abstractions, a white square on a white ground, a feat which not even Kandinsky, Mondrian or Kupka could achieve, it is still preferable to refer to the artist's writings.

For Malevich Cubism, which had been derived from Cézanne's revolutionary ideas, was the decisive factor:

The Cubists, thanks to the pulverisation of the object, left the field of objectivity, and this moment marked the beginning of pure painterly culture. Painterly texture is beginning to flourish, as such, and not the object but colour and painting are coming onto the scene. Cubism is freeing the artist from dependence on the creative forms of nature and technology that surround him, and placing him on the absolute, inventive, directly creative path.[47]

Futurism is credited with having renewed the themes and not the dynamics of the modern world, but however, "the efforts of Futurism to provide a pure painterly plasticity have not been crowned with success; it could not separate itself from figurative aspects in general and could only destroy objects in the name of a new dynamic form."[48] Malevich found the cubo-futurist efforts rather faint-hearted: "The Cubo-Futurists piled objects in the main square and destroyed them, but they did not burn them. Pity!"[49] For Malevich true painterly realism was "painting for its own sake"; but it was not a question of confronting this new realism with the copy or the transposition of the real: "Creation only exists in paintings which contain a form which borrows nothing from what has been created in Nature, but which is derived from painterly masses and which neither repeats nor modifies the basic forms of objects in nature."[50] This marks the dividing line between Malevich and Kan-

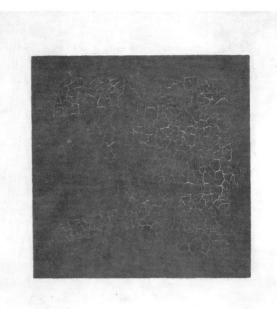

Black Square, 1914–15. Oil on canvas, 31¼×31¼ in. (79.5×79.5 cm). State Tretyakov Gallery, Moscow.

dinsky. The author of *Concerning the Spiritual in Art* rejects copies of the material world and any personal object which might interfere with the painting in order to concentrate more fully on the spiritual world and describe the objects of an interior world which represented the most interesting aspects of nature for Kandinsky: "If we begin at once to break the bonds which bind us to nature, and devote ourselves purely to combination of pure colour and abstract form, we shall produce works which are mere decoration, which are suited to neckties or carpets."[51] This is totally different from Suprematism as defined by Malevich in the 1919 Non-Objective Creation and Suprematist Exhibition catalogue: "The system is constructed in time and space, independently of all aesthetic beauties, experiences or moods: it is more a philosophical colour system for realizing the latest achievements of my ideas, as knowledge."[52] In an unpublished text dating from the 1920s, Malevich seems to be replying to certain of the statements made by Kandinsky; he affirms that: "Suprematism is also a prism, but the prism through which one does not see a single 'what.' In the suprematist prism the world is beyond limit, in its prism 'the world' of things is not refracted, for they do not exist, they are non-objective."[53]

Malevich chose the term Suprematism to express the radicalism of his new work where the purity of painting attained its most advanced state. Historians have noted how this word is derived from the Latin *suprematia* rather than from the Russian. Larissa Zhadova has pointed out that this word also exists in another language which Malevich knew well, Polish. In September 1915, while Malevich was working on his first pamphlet on Suprematism, he explained his choice of term to his friend Matiushin: "It seems to me that Suprematism is the most suitable [term], since it signifies dominance."[54] This idea of dominance escaped most of the critics present at the 0.10 exhibition. B. Lopatin wrote: "Barrenness, monotony, there is no painting and no individuality in the Suprematists";[55] but it was an article by Alexandre Benois which most outraged Malevich, who responded in a violent and ironic letter: "But it is difficult for you to get warm at the face of a square, accustomed as you are to get your warmth from a sweet little face. . . . For the secret of the incantation is the art of creation itself, and it lies in time, time which is greater and wiser than swine!"[56] However, Malevich's friends and followers were enthusiastic. A hint of Malevich's ideas can be found in Khlebnikov's writings when he expresses the desire to

speak of time before any measure for it was available, using only a bucket of paint. And so the face of time was painted in words on the old canvases of the Koran, the Vedas, the Gospels, and other doctrines. That great face is adumbrated here also in the pure Laws of Time, but this time with the brush of number, and thus we take a different approach to the task of our predecessors. The canvas contains no words, only precise number, which functions here as the artist's brushstroke depicting the face of time.[57]

The reference to sacred texts which forbade the representation of the human figure is also present in the writings of other theorists of abstract painting, particularly Kupka. Of all the abstractionist theorists, Malevich was closer to Kupka than to any other; their spiritualism derived from the theosophy invoked by Kandinsky and Mondrian as well as from Herbin's interpretation of the anthroposophist doctrine of Steiner.

The extent of the suprematist idiom became visible from the moment of the 0.10 exhibition; the system was conceived without reference to any form of nature and was based on flat elementary geometrical figures (quadrilaterals, triangles and circles) and sustained colour which were combined with impressive formal inventiveness. The forms were never simply decorative and go against Kandinsky's statement on the dangers of breaking "the bonds which bind us to nature." In order to demonstrate the richness of the paintings, several dating from 1915 are described briefly below; they range from the most complex of constructions to the simplest monochrome figure. The combinations are almost infinite and depend on the number and form of figures, the diversity of colours and whether the figures overlap partially or stand freely:

Supremus No. 50. A number of rectangles, almost rectangular trapezia and small triangles overlap or stand freely. The large figures are of two dominant colours: red and black. The smaller quadrilaterals are of three colours: three are yellow, one is violet and two discrete oblong rectangles are deep blue.

Suprematism. A large black quadrilateral dominates the composition; it is surrounded and partly covered by red, violet, blue, green, yellow and orange rectangles, some of which are so thin they resemble pieces of ribbon.

Suprematism: Painterly Realism of a Soccer Player. The pictorial space is dominated by two groups of elements: a single parallelogram and a contrasting archipelago of seven forms (three unequal black, yellow and blue overlapping quadrilaterals, three red and black rectangles and a blue circle).

Suprematism: Self-Portrait in Two Dimensions (pl. 35). A centrally positioned black square in the top half of the canvas dominates five isolated or touching but not overlapping figures: a blue trapezium touches a black rectangle, a yellow rectangle touches a brown square in the proximity of a brown ring. Overlapping figures generally give the impression of a collage, that is, of cutout shapes applied over each other; however, in this canvas the two dimensional qualities of the painting prevail.

Suprematism (with Eight Red Rectangles). Eight freestanding, almost regular, red rectangles float in a cluster. They seem to be engaged in almost parallel, diagonal flight across the canvas.

Suprematism (with Blue Triangle and Black Rectangle). Only two large forms and contrasting colours are depicted here: a blue triangle partially buried in a black square. El Lissitzky must have remembered the startlingly simple dynamic effect of this canvas when in 1920 he designed the famous propaganda poster *Beat the Whites with the Red Wedge.*

Malevich further simplified the use of forms in *Red Square: Painterly Realism of a Peasant Woman in Two Dimensions.* Only one form (a square) and one colour (red) occupy the centre of this square canvas. The famous *Black Square* (pl. 31), though based on the same principles, would be considered ostensibly more elementary and therefore more shocking by visitors to the 0.10 exhibition, no doubt because black and white are seldom considered to be true colours. Many painters from Malevich to Herbin have refuted this.

All elementary suprematist forms are derived from the square: the rectangle by stretching, the circle by rotation and the cross by vertical and horizontal translation (*Black Cross* and *Black Circle* are the companion forms of *Black Square*). *Black Square* (pl. 31) always epitomized suprematist aesthetics, both for Malevich and the public. The artist painted several versions of this canvas at different moments of his career, and the painting opened his funeral procession and was placed on his tomb; for these reasons, it warrants closer study.

In his letter to Alexandre Benois, Malevich defined his *Black Square* as "a single bare and frameless icon of our times,"[58] the icon of its time, or to reemploy Khlebnikov's expression, "the face of time." The intention to present *Black Square* as a new icon was obvious at the 0.10 exhibition because it was hung in a corner of the gallery close to the ceiling in the "place of honour," the place where the family icon is displayed in traditional orthodox homes and where people look upon entering and make the sign of the cross. But no undue symbolic interpretation should be attributed to it. It is relevant to quote Ouspensky's words on the *Lao Tzu:* "The Tao is a great square with no angles . . . a great sound which cannot be heard, a great image with no form."[59] Whether Malevich was familiar with this text or not is uncertain. Although *Black Square* is not a mystical or anarchist emblem, he could not help thinking about it when he wrote: "Anarchy is coloured black, i.e. in a dark colour, we do not see a single differentiation — a dark ray has swallowed up all the colours and has placed everything beyond variations and advantages, everything is the same: colourless dark."[60] If we insist on finding a meaning at all costs, we become immersed in a type of symbolic interpretation which Malevich condemned. *Black Square,* like all other suprematist works, has no other meaning than itself both in relation to itself and to the work of Malevich, his development and his economy of form. However, it should be pointed out that at one stage, Malevich proposed *Black Square* as a revolutionary sign, and *Black Cross* as the sign of his death, indicating that it was difficult not to be influenced by the conventional association of ideas on forms and colours; it should

Supremus N.º 50, 1915. Oil on canvas, 38¼×26 in. (97×66 cm). Stedelijk Museum, Amsterdam.

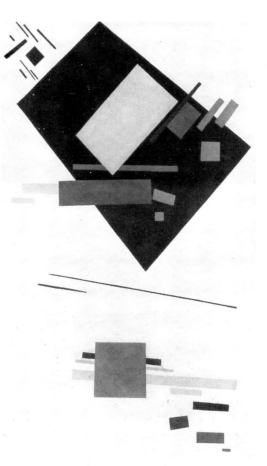

Suprematism, 1915. Oil on canvas, 40×24⅜ in. (101.5×62 cm). Stedelijk Museum, Amsterdam.

Suprematism: Painterly Realism of a Soccer Player, 1915. Oil on canvas, 27⅝×17⅛ in. (70×44 cm). Stedelijk Museum, Amsterdam.

nevertheless be emphasized that *a priori Black Square* does not signify anything. It simply exists.

A point in common between the Wanderers and their opponents the Symbolists was their preoccupation for non-painterly concerns; the plight of the masses for the former group and metaphysics for the latter. The young artist had adhered to both ideas and Cubism and Futurism must have seemed very formal by comparison. However, occurring after Cubism and Futurism, the suprematist square, though non-symbolic, suggested ideas not related to the painting since it made reference to the medieval icon.

Close study of the development of *Black Square* shows that Malevich did not arrive directly at the mono-chromatic square. The paint of the first version which dates from 1915 (*Black Suprematist Square,* State Tretya-kov Gallery), has unfortunately cracked over time. The cracks allow the slightest of traces of earlier paint (red, blue, green and other undefinable colours) to show through under the black. Further examination under an oblique source of light reveals infinitely small differences in the thickness of the paint and the intensity of the col-our; traces of a large trapezium and two secant triangles can also be discerned under the paint. It would seem that Malevich, in order to take his painterly reflections to their extreme culmination, painted his black square over an earlier more complicated but infinitely less radical suprematist work. Certain critics would go as far as to say that the fact that an earlier painting has been covered by *Black Square* is highly significant.

The full title of *Red Square: Painterly Realism of a Pea-sant Woman in Two Dimensions* (pl. 34) makes reference

Suprematism (with Eight Red Rectangles), 1915.
Oil on canvas, 22⅗ × 19⅛ in. (57.5 × 48.5 cm). Stedelijk Museum, Amsterdam.

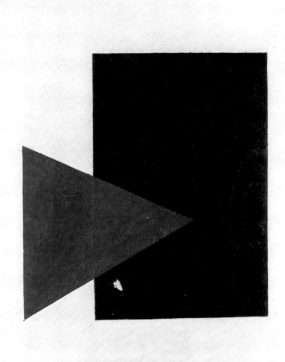

Suprematism (with Blue Triangle and Black Rectangle), 1915.
Oil on canvas, 26¼ × 22½ in. (66.5 × 57 cm). Stedelijk Museum, Amsterdam.

to external reality. *Black Square,* a strictly retinal painting, can only refer to itself, hence the fascination it exercised for painters like Yves Klein. The fact that it should be called "square" is nothing but convention, a highly debatable convenience. The exact Russian word that Malevich chose to describe it was *quadrangle;* nothing in the word implies parallelism or sides of equal length or right angles. In fact, Malevich's square is not exactly square: this is sensed simply by observing it and proved by measuring it. Similarly, *Black Cross* (pl. 33) is a St. George's cross with arms of unequal length (especially the 1915 version) and *Black Circle* (pl. 32) is not centrally positioned on its white field.

It is no less important that *Black Square* should have been noticeably painted in free hand; despite much restoration work, the surface of the square still reveals the brush strokes. Unlike many of the geometrical abstract painters, Malevich never used drawing instruments or perfectly uniform colour; he wanted the imperfections of the human hand to be seen in the slight irregularities of the sides of the square.

Malevich insisted that his painting was "a single bare and frameless icon" which is why, as the photograph of the 0.10 exhibition of 1915 reveals, his black, frameless quadrangle was hung obliquely in a corner near the ceiling — as if it were to be understood and revered in a manner similar to icons in traditional orthodox homes. For some time now, these hanging requirements have been ignored. Like all other paintings, *Black Square* is now shown in a wooden frame, and far from being an icon it is displayed on a flat wall.

Shortly after *Black Square,* Malevich painted its opposite, a white square. But *Red Square* also presents a very particular case. If the symbolism of the colour is excluded (especially in the light of the Revolution), it is useful to bear in mind a simple fact which is not apparent

from the simple translation; in Russian, the word for "red" and "beautiful" is the same; in fact Moscow's Red Square bore this name long before the Revolution because it happened to be the most beautiful square in the city. That the *Red Square* is also the *Beautiful Square* dispenses with the need for blue or green squares.

Malevich had opened up the way for the color-field painters of the 1950s. Later, by painting other versions of his square at different stages of his career (sometimes his students executed the copies) he was opening the field of speculation as to whether several copies of one work of art could be produced and as to whether the originality of a creator lay in the execution of his own work. One can also argue endlessly whether the black and red colours of the squares are retinal (for the simple pleasure of the eye) or metaphoric (the transposition of a peasant woman, an anarchist flag, etc., onto canvas), but in each case, including *Suprematist Composition: White on White,* they are not "the last painting" of a series as Rodchenko wished his own monochromatic compositions to be. For Malevich, the square was the result from which all further development could proceed or be reconsidered, whether it was in painting, sculpture, architectonics, applied arts or even writing. Only after having wiped clean the tablets could there be a rebirth. In his enthusiastic lecture, *New Russian Art* (1922), Malevich's most talented disciple, El Lissitzky, clearly outlined the significance of his master's square:

In 1913 Malevich exhibited a black square painted on a white canvas. Here a form was displayed which was opposed to everything that was understood by "picture" or "painting" or "art." Its creator wanted to reduce all forms, all painting to zero. For us however, this zero was the turning point. When we have a series of numbers coming from infinity . . . 6, 5, 4, 3, 2, 1, 0 . . . it comes right down to the zero and then begins the ascending line 0, 1, 2, 3, 4, 5, 6 . . .[61]

SUPREMATISM AND THE REVOLUTION

The technical observations made above about *Black Square* apply to all of Malevich's suprematist paintings. Exception should be made of the titles of works where the artist's attitude has changed: the first suprematist titles make reference to an external reality and probably contain a certain touch of provocative humour, e.g. *Painterly Realism of a Soccer Player* or *Self-Portrait in Two Dimensions* (pl. 35), but these rapidly give way to more neutral titles like *Blue Triangle and Black Rectangle* and *Black Circle* or to series which are simply numbered (e.g. *Supremus No. 50* and *Supremus No. 56*, etc.). Malevich does not attach any symbolic relevance to colour, unlike Kandinsky; the colour is always uniform and without shadow or tone as the paintings are two dimensional, but it is not applied to the canvas particularly meticulously. All of the coloured forms are presented whole and none are mutilated by the edges of the canvas; thus the painting presents a self-contained universe, a whole. In this respect, Suprematism is the antithesis of the neo-plastic work of Mondrian which is defined by its "absence of limited form."[62] Although the forms are geometrical, the edges are sometimes shaky and it is not unusual for the pencilled outlines to show through from underneath. The finish of the works retains the barely perceptible trembling of the artist's hand, and this human touch balances the coldness which is all too often attributed to Malevich's work.

Exhibiting Malevich's suprematist paintings today poses many problems: the fashion of the time for walls cluttered with three or four rows of irregularly-sized paintings has passed; additionally it is not always clear which is the top or the bottom of a canvas. Even in Malevich's day and in exhibitions which he himself helped to mount, a painting may have been hung in more than one position. The specialists T. Andersen and N. Khardzhiev argue for one or another solution and at the 1989 retrospective held in Moscow and Amsterdam there were at least three cases where the catalogue photograph and the exhibited work were presented in different positions. It could be argued, as Ouspensky claimed, that "there is nothing which is right or left, or below or above" but this is pure rhetoric when one is faced with the practical problem of hanging the paintings. Once again, it would be useful to refer to Malevich who gave some thought to the hanging of works in his text "The Axis of Colour and Form" (1919): "Museum walls are flat surfaces on which works should be placed in the same order as the composition of forms is placed on the pictural surface."[63] Any person who has had the responsibility for organizing an exhibition knows that the place and relative position of a painting is of the greatest importance both for the individual work and for the overall effect of the exhibition. If Malevich's reasoning is followed, and if the wall or walls become artistic compositions in themselves, this would mean that depending on the works available for exhibition it would be possible to turn one painting or another onto its side for the sake of the overall composition. In discussions of this kind, personal preferences should be avoided and wherever the artist has left any indications, for example, his signature or notes on the back of the canvas, these should be respected and the painting hung accordingly.

As soon as the first Suprematist works became known, a section of the artistic avant-garde immediately adhered to the movement; these artists included younger painters like Ivan Puni and Olga Rozanova and even Kliun who was six years Malevich's senior. Malevich's own artistic and theoretical following is worth mentioning: in 1933 Nikolai Suetin, one of his disciples, wrote about him with as much enthusiasm as on the first day: "The square is a phenomenon of Russian art which will prove to be of world importance, as it proved to be for myself. The square can be compared with the Egyptian sphinx and it continues to form part of the inheritance of all cultures which paint icons."[64] This was an accurate prediction as the square has indeed enjoyed a prosperous future in western art, even without considering the other artistic directions which it took, including the De Stijl movement and Josef Albers. Almost half a century after Suetin's declaration, Victor Vasarely wrote the following about Malevich's square: "These canvases are, in my opinion, the symbol of a great turning point in modern art, and the perfect illustration of the end of macroscopic possibilities on a flat plane. One could not illustrate more clearly the imperative need to paint something else."[65] Malevich and the Suprematists sought that "something else" so eagerly that they would completely abandon easel painting.

In 1916 preparations were being made for the publication of the first issue of the magazine *Supremus;* Malevich held the position of editor and Olga Rozanova that of editorial secretary. In a letter written by Rozanova to Matiushin requesting an article in the field of music, she explains:

The magazine is a periodical. It is strictly of the party in character. Its programme is: Suprematism in painting, sculpture, architecture, music, the new theatre etc. . . . Articles of a scientific and artistic-scientific nature etc. . . . Contributors to the magazine, the members of the *Supremus* Society: Udaltsova, Popova, Kliun, Menkov, Pestel, Archipenko, Davidova, Rozanova, etc. Editor of the magazine: Malevich. Poets: Kruchenykh, Aliagrov and others.[66]

Unfortunately the magazine never appeared, largely due to the upheaval connected with the Revolution, but the description of the project illustrates the all-embracing interests of the Suprematists. The programmes which Kandinsky and Mondrian proposed also included not only painting but music, poetry, theatre and the decorative arts. It is not certain what Malevich understood by suprematist music, but his ideas on poetry were perfectly clear. In *On Poetry* (1919), he explained: "I consider the highest moment in the poet's service of the spirit to be that of his wordless dialect, when demented words rush from his mouth, mad words accessible neither to the mind, nor to reason,"[67] in other words the *zaum*, the transrational language used by Khlebnikov and Krutchenykh and later by Aliagrov, pseudonym of the linguist Roman Jakobson. The recently formed Russian School of formalist linguists showed a lasting interest in the *zaum* and in the first steps of Suprematism. Victor Shklovski revealed the relationship between the different fields: "The Suprematists did for art what chemistry has done for medicine: they have isolated the active factor in the remedies."[68]

From the fifteenth century onwards, the development of perspective which subsequently dominated the arts was mirrored in the establishment of a strong central power which would rule over the states of Europe for several centuries. This is more than just mere coincidence. In Tsarist Russia, the established order felt under vague threat when the questions of perspective and consequently of figurative representation were called into question. They had hitherto been accepted unquestioningly and their undermining seemed to be related in some undefined way to the opposition to the centralized government. Consequently, Cubists, Futurists and any other persons found to be abusing the sacrosanct conventions of perspective and syntax were frowned upon by official Tsarist authorities.

When the Revolution broke out in 1917 all the writers and artists whom the public had disparagingly designated as "futurists" immediately took up its cause. They were hoping for the overthrow of the established order against which they had been fighting for years. Malevich, like his friends, was never an aesthete who lived in isolation from the problems of his time. Already in the autumn of 1914 he had contributed a number of propaganda posters to the war effort. They were executed in the rough, unpolished and highly coloured style of the folk *lubok* and exalted the victories of Russia, symbolized by the peasant; they invariably included a short satirical verse which told, for example, of how when "The Austrian went to Radziwill, he fell on the peasant woman's pitchfork." 1917 and the Revolution provided a particularly important and fundamental stake for them. There were many who like Mayakovsky called for the birth of the new revolutionary man. Kamensky's "Decree" on painting, poetry and music which was posted all over Moscow in the first days of Soviet power gave some of the idea of the enthusiasm which the artists carried with them:

Poets!
Take your brushes and go.
With a ladder paste your
Posters, your sheets full of verses,
To the walls.
Tell the truth about life,
Behave in the eyes of life like a boyfriend
In front of his girl.

Painters!
Big Burliuks,
Go towards the houses in carnival spirit,
Liven up the colours of your paintings,
Take packets of posters,
Paint the walls and the squares
And the signs and the shop windows with genius.

Malevich contributed to the Revolution in his own way. In 1918, he published a series of seven militant articles in the magazine *Anarkhia* (*Anarchy*); the anarchists had played a very active role in the Revolution before being progressively eliminated: "The social revolution which smashed the chains of capitalist slavery has not yet smashed the old tables of aesthetic values. And now, as the new building and creation of cultural values is commencing, it is essential to guard oneself against the poison of bourgeois banality."[69] The idea that the aesthetic revolution and the armed revolution were inseparable was very dear to Malevich. He returned to it in his essay "The Question of Imitative Art" (1921) where declarations like the following seemed to outline his actions for the coming years: "The movement of the new world is divided in two: on the one hand the fighting destructive avant-garde with the banner of economics, politics, right and freedom, and, on the other the creative army which appears after it, creating form for the whole utilitarian and spiritual world of things."[70] The importance of changing the world was clear to Malevich, but this change was closer to Bakunin's idea than to Marx's:

We wish to form ourselves according to a new pattern, plan and system; we wish to build in such a way that all the elements of nature will unite with man and create a single, all-powerful image. . . . Thus every personality, every individual, formerly isolated, is now incorporated in the system of united action.[71]

Malevich was a visionary of an anarcho-communist Utopia which the harsh realities of the 1920s and 1930s would inevitably disappoint: "The communist town is not arising from the chaos of private buildings, but according to a general plan and not from the whim of individual personalities."[72] This desire to work on a general plan for the good of the greatest number of individuals was implicit in all the team work which he undertook. In reality, Malevich's most lasting influence was not as a political thinker, but rather the man proclaimed "Chairman of the World" by the Russian pre-Revolutionary avant-garde, Khlebnikov himself. Malevich's conviction that "the cages of nationalities, fatherlands and nations [should] be destroyed in a revolutionary manner" and that "the organization of a single human state, or a non-state, material, cultural plantation"[73] was desirable, expressed in "On New Systems in Art" (1919) and in "The Question of Imitative Art" (1921), undoubtedly derived from Khlebnikov. In *War in a Mousetrap* (1915–17), Khlebnikov denounced the government of old people which oppressed youth and sent it to its death; Malevich echoed this idea:

If only the state would look around and see the absurdity of these stiflings; they would see that not merely are all things they stifled alive, but that a whole youthful world is growing from them. Babies proliferate whilst the old state pours soldiers into the streets to exterminate them; in each young thing it seeks out the living principle in order to kill it. This is as much the practice in art as in political life. But nothing comes of it since youth is immortal; safeguarded by life it moves towards its inevitable growth, the finiteness which is defined in itself and the affirmation and completion of the established stage of forms in the world's perfection.[74]

This was not simply a piece of youthful bravado, Malevich was at the height of his powers when he wrote it. His fundamental optimism has never been sufficiently emphasized. Rather like Khlebnikov's utopian writings, e.g. *Roar about the Railroads* (1914),[75] Malevich's writings affirm his belief in technical progress (the train, the aeroplane and the automobile had already captivated the Futurists) and in the fact that nature could be perfected through human intervention:

Nature groans in defeat, for my legs which were given me by it are nothing by comparison with the wheels that I myself have created. The train will take me and my baggage around the earth at the speed of lightning. My communications with other towns

Two propaganda posters ("The Austrian went to Radziwill" and "What a Boom, what a Blast"), 1914. Lithographs, 12⅞×19½ in. (32.8×49.5 cm). State Russian Museum, Leningrad.

will be easy and convenient. I shall make my whole state comfortable and convenient, and, what is more, I shall convert other states and eventually the whole globe to my comfort and convenience.[76]

Malevich's optimism was the basis for all his actions as artist and theorist that he was and for the pedagogue which he was to become.

Malevich was not so naïve as to believe that all his idealistic ideas could be fulfilled without a struggle. He knew all too well that for years he had been hurling himself against the wall of public and official conservatism and that his ideas would have trouble imposing themselves against established ideas, in art perhaps more than in any other domain. He knew he would have to take into account the backwardness of public opinion and, even worse, the backwardness of its official representatives in the government. Malevich criticized the Bolshevik officials, and in particular the Commissar of Education, Lunacharsky, who had a very low opinion of Suprematism:

People always demand that art be comprehensible, but they never demand of themselves that they adapt their mind to comprehension; even the most cultured socialists have taken the same line and make the same demands of art as a merchant asking a painter to make him a signboard showing in a comprehensible manner the goods available in his shop. And many people, especially socialists, think that art exists for the purpose of painting comprehensible buns.[77]

On top of this somewhat short-sighted utilitarianism, the cultural officials based their aesthetic ideals on styles which had long been surpassed, this was probably due to their lack of fundamental artistic taste rather than to any desire for demagogy: "and if the specialists also raise a hue and cry in the papers and journals against the formations of new conclusions in art, it is because within them still lives the art by which public opinion lived before the socialist era."[78] If Malevich, the "great idealist of liberty," to quote Luis Cardoza y Aragón, was still a long way from having imposed his new ideas on Suprematism, this does not mean that the Bolshevik government had deprived him of his means of action: the state had entrusted him with a number of artistic missions, at least for the near future.

Malevich was obviously on the side of the Revolution, and he was appointed to a number of official functions.

From 1917 to 1919 he was given the responsibility of overseeing the restructuring of the national art collections and of artistic education; during this time he continued to paint. In 1918 he and Matiushin were commissioned to execute a mural for the Congress of the Committee on Rural Poverty in Petrograd; he was also commissioned to design the set for the grand performance of Mayakovsky's *Mystery Bouff*, dedicated to the Revolution. Malevich must have been pleased to see art in a much wider context than just museums and galleries and out of the hands of collectors and curators in such settings as these where a very wide audience could enjoy it. He continued to experiment further: one canvas, *Suprematist Painting: Yellow Quadrilateral on White* (1917–18, pl. 46), shows a yellow quadrilateral with one side merging into the infinity of the white ground. 1918 was the memorable year in which he painted a series of white paintings on white grounds, the most remarkable being *Suprematist Composition: White on White* (pl. 55). For Malevich this was the logical outcome of his research:

Suprematism is divided into three stages according to the number of black, red and white squares: the black, coloured and white periods. . . . The three squares of Suprematism represent the establishment of definite types of *Weltanschauung* and world building. The white square is a purely economic movement of the form, which embodies the whole new white world building. . . . In the community they [the three squares] have received another significance: the black one as a sign of economy, the red one as the signal for revolution, and the white one as pure action.[79]

When he exhibited his white paintings at the national exhibition in Moscow ("Non-Figurative Art and Suprematism") in 1919, he rejoiced: "I have torn through the blue lamp shade of colour limitations, and come out into the white; after me, comrade aviators, sail into the chasm. . . . Sail forth! The white, free chasm, infinity is before us."[80] Rather than being a nihilist gesture as certain persons believed, the white paintings (and especially more so as Rodchenko had exhibited *Black on Black* at the same exhibition) were the supreme exaltation of painting and of the *act of painting*. In the white square as in the other white paintings it is the technique which creates the form; it is the individual brush strokes and the varying thickness of the white paint and not the intensity of the white which make the white figures stand out from their white backgrounds.

Despite his discoveries and his temperament of a born leader, Malevich was not the undisputed master of the Russian avant-garde. He had a rival, Tatlin, who was also a fertile inventor (the *Counter-reliefs*) and prince of the rising constructivist movement. Nikolai Punin delighted in making ironic comments in *Iskusstvo kommuny*, a magazine which had previously published work by Malevich: "Suprematism has blossomed out in splendid colour all over Moscow. Posters, exhibitions, cafés — all is Suprematism," he went on to praise Tatlin for having defined Suprematism as "simply the sum of past errors but nevertheless acknowledges a future for it in the applied and decorative arts."[81] However, even if he was at loggerheads with Kliun, and even if some of the most prominent Suprematists like Popova had begun to drift away, Malevich still continued to fascinate and draw young talents towards himself. Neither the rising constructivist movement nor the official aversion of the State to Suprematism deprived Malevich of a significant following. It is perhaps El Lissitzky in "New Russian Art" who best expresses the debt of the younger artists to their master: "we pay tribute to the courage of he who threw himself into the chasm in order to rise again from the dead under a new form."

For Malevich, easel painting seemed to have arrived at its logical conclusion, at least provisionally. In 1920, he summarized the achievements of Suprematism in his work *Suprematism: 34 Drawings*, which appeared, significantly, at the Vitebsk Unovis (College of New Art) workshop, where Malevich had just taken up his functions as professor. In the foreword he announced that he was abandoning easel painting in order to devote himself to the theory and pedagogical methodology of art and to writing. It was an extremely important turning point in his career, and he had absolutely no doubt about it:

The economic question has become for me the principal pinnacle from which I look down and examine all the creations of the material world: this work with pen rather than brush is my chief occupation. It seems that one cannot attain with a brush what can be attained with a pen. It is tousled and cannot get into the inner reaches of the brain — the pen is finer.... There can be no question of painting in Suprematism; painting was done for long ago, and the artist himself is a prejudice of the past.... Having established definite plans for the Suprematist system, I place the further development of architectural Suprematism in the hands of the young architects, in the broad sense of the word, for in this alone do I see an epoch with a new system of architecture.[82]

By placing easel painting firmly in the past, Malevich was replying to Tatlin and, by anticipation, to the Constructivists. In the first issue of *Iskusstvo kommuny* (December 1918), Ossip Brik gave artists new directions in which to construct Socialism; after having denounced the "ideological sleep" of artists, he professed:

Factories, works and workshops are waiting for artists to come and to give them models of new objects which have never been seen.... We need to organize institutes of material culture where artists will prepare to work on the creation of new everyday objects for the proletarians, and where objects of this type, the works of art of the future, will be developed.[83]

While retaining his autonomy in relation to the growing trend in Constructivism, Malevich was putting his art at the service of "social demand" by orienting Suprematism towards theory in order to shake it from its slumbers and above all towards architecture (applied to buildings and to ordinary objects) which was an immediately useful form of art in a country undergoing full reconstruction following the founding of the new political regime. It is more than significant that Malevich should have rewritten one of his earlier manifestos which had appeared in *Anarkhia* for the issue of *Iskusstvo kommuny* which carried Brik's manifesto. In it, Malevich vehemently recommended that outmoded architecture be shelved and that a new architecture, liberated from the past, replace it:

Our new architect will be he who, throwing aside Greece and Rome, speaks in the new language of architecture. Ruined towns await your miracles, your new ideas. But, for God's sake do not turn up with the covers of old bibles and testaments. But we painters must rise to the defence of new buildings, and, for the time being, lock up or even blow up the institute of old architects; we must burn the remains of the Greeks in the crematorium, to impel people towards what is new, in order that the newly forged image of our day be pure.[84]

While the foreword of *Suprematism, 34 Drawings* summarized Suprematism and its new perspectives, the work also marked the birth of Unovis. The text ends with a loud and energetic rallying cry: "Long live Unovis, creating and affirming what is new in the world."[85] Unovis was a typically Russian abbreviation of "uchilishche novovo iskusstva," affirmation (or affirmers) of the new art. From September 1920, Malevich taught at the Vitebsk School of Art. Vitebsk was an important artistic capital in Byelorussia and also happened to be the birthplace of Marc Chagall, which was the main reason why Lunacharsky had entrusted him with the direction of the School of Art; but Chagall and Malevich could never understand each other or work together. Suprematism, which had the full support of the most prominent faculty members (El Lissitzky, Vera Ermolaeva and Ilya Chashnik), soon won the day. When Malevich's new plan for collective artistic work, Unovis, was approved in 1920, Chagall resigned and Malevich occupied his post. Thus, it was under the sign of Suprematism that Vitebsk celebrated the third anniversary of the October Revolution; brightly coloured geometrical forms were erected at crossroads, in the main thoroughfares, on walls and on buses and trams. Malevich and his colleagues worked frenetically on their collective projects. Lissitzky would say: "For us Suprematism did not signify the recognition of an absolute form which was part of an already-completed universal system; on the contrary here stood revealed for the first time in all its purity the clear sign and plan for a definite new world never before experienced."[86] In several of the texts and manifestos issued by Unovis, Malevich affirmed his desire to work in agreement with the Communist Party and with the same perspectives in view: "New art is no longer organized under the flag of aesthetic taste, but is passing over to party organization. Unovis is now a party which has put economy as its basis. Thus art becomes closely linked with the communism of humanity's economic well-being."[87] This type of statement could be found in declarations made by all Russian artistic and literary circles of the time, whether by opportunism or by conviction, but a man as alien to demagogy as Malevich almost certainly approved of the objectives of the Revolution in its infancy. He wanted the artist to abandon his studio and to work with other artists and artisans for the good of the community. He broke down the barriers between the fine arts and applied arts within Unovis: "All workshops should be equal, be they painters', tailors' or potters'. They should see in everything a single unity and mutual dependence as well as a coherence in the unity of the organism."[88] In its revolutionary Utopianism, the creative committee of Unovis wanted to embrace not only the artists but also the artisans and the workers of the whole world:

Youths of the West, the East and the South, go towards the red pole of the new earth, since that is where burns the flag of the new art. For action, votes and movement we call not only on those responsible for the arts, but also upon our comrades — the smiths, fitters, braziers, concrete pourers, foundry men, carpenters, machinists, aviators, stone cutters, miners, textile workers, tailors, dressmakers and all who make useful things in the world at large so that under the common flag of the UNOVIS we may together dress the earth in clothes of new shape and purpose.[89]

These declarations are not far removed from those of the Constructivists (and in this respect Andrei Nakov cleverly makes the parallel between the Unovis and the Constructivists in his book *Abstrait/Concret: Art non-objectif Russe et Polonais*). Nevertheless, Suprematism aroused a number of hostile comments from the Moscow Constructivists and Productivists who criticized it for over-concentrating on research rather than working on practical and utilitarian projects. The Vitebsk municipal authorities, who failed to grasp the significance of Suprematism, began to have doubts about Unovis, and in 1922 the Constructivists of the Moscow Institute of Painterly Culture (INKhUK) refused their support and Unovis had to leave for Petrograd (the new name of St. Petersburg, later Leningrad) where it was welcomed by the Petrograd State Institute for Painterly Culture. Malevich was full of hope, especially as a number of highly talented professors and students including Ermolaeva, Chashnik, Suetin, Lev Yudin and Lazare Khiedekel had made the move with him.

This was a particularly busy moment in the life and career of Malevich, although few works from this period have survived (pl. 55, 56). Troels Andersen has summarized it very succinctly:

He devoted all of his energy to theoretical work and experiment in architectonics. To the best of our knowledge no new paintings or sketches were produced around the mid-twenties. Pedagogical research was another of his daily tasks. He was also involved in a considerable amount of administrative work during the first years after the Revolution.[90]

Fortunately, the time he devoted to his writing, teaching and administrative tasks did not prevent him from directing practical research work in teams where architecture and not painting would be at the centre of his theory.

ARCHITEKTONS AND GINKhUK

Malevich never neglected architecture, but in the post-revolutionary years, after having abandoned painting, he saw in architecture the possible synthesis of all other arts: "Architectural work is an art of synthesis, that is why it should become associated with all domains of art."[91] Suprematism had shown an interest in three-dimensional work from the moment of its first public exhibition in 1915; indeed Kliun had exhibited suprematist sculptures made of geometrical solids, but the rigorous work of Malevich and his team of Unovis artists was still a long way off.

Malevich began work on what he called the *Planits* (pls. 57, 58, 59), architectural projects which were executed as three-dimensional cardboard models but of which only drawings and plans on paper have survived. As their name suggests, the *Planits* were inhabitable structures which gravitated in space like tiny planets (today they would be called sputniks or space stations). Some of them could also be placed on the ground or on water. The structures were made up of different sized parallelepipeds assembled as a harmonious whole. These floating towns, which had earlier been part of Khlebnikov's dream, formed part of the Russian artistic tradition of the 1920s in the same way as Tatlin's monumental *Tower* or Krutikov's aerial living quarters. Though they were utopian and impossible to construct, Malevich's *Planits* were nevertheless imagined down to fine detail. On one drawing of a *Planit* (1924) he noted the following: "I am now thinking about the materials — matt white glass, concrete, roofing felt, electric heating without chimneys for *Planits*. A live *Planit* is mainly coloured black and white. Red, black and white in exceptional cases."[92] During his period of residence at Vitebsk, Malevich would "come down to Earth" with a new field of research which was more in keeping with the technological potential of his day: the *Architektons* (pls. 60, 61, 62). The word, which he had defined in several ways, was a neologism coined from architectonics; in "Painting and the Problem of Architecture," published in *Nova Generatsiya* (1928), it was defined as: "architectural formulae with the aid of which one can give form to architectural structures."[93] Depending on the desired dynamic effect, the *Architektons* were vertical or horizontal constructions which were placed on the ground, they were monumental living quarters. As with the *Planits*, the square was the basis of the design; by translating squares of different sizes a variety of cubic volumes or parallelepipeds were obtained. Jean-Hubert Martin has suggested from photographic evidence that the first *Architektons* were made of cardboard, and from 1923 onwards of plaster (and very rarely of wood and glass).[94] Several of the original *Architektons* have been conserved and restored. What was surprising about these sky-scrapers of the 1920s was the extraordinary inventiveness which had gone into their design and the diversity of solutions imagined from parallelepipeds of greatly differing sizes, which range from 2 millimetres to almost one metre in some of the models. Malevich did not use preconstructed or prefabricated elements which could be adapted to one construction or another; each *Architekton* was assembled from elements which were exclusive to itself and which were based on the intuition of the architect or architects and not according to mathematical formulae, as was the case with the contemporary work of Georges Vantongerloo and the De Stijl neoplastic movement.

As in the *Planits,* colour played an important role in the *Architektons;* Malevich repeatedly affirmed that colour influenced form and changed space.[95] Several models for *Architektons* contain a circle, a square or a cross painted onto the structure or painted on glass which is then laid into the plaster (e.g. the plaster and glass *Black Cross* at the Centre Pompidou, Paris), but most of the complete *Architektons* (or fragments) which have survived are completely white; some bear slight traces of colour which would appear to have been removed at some stage of their development. It would seem that the *Architektons* underwent the same colour evolution as suprematist painting, from black and white to colour (with a marked preference for red) and finally to overall white. It is also true, as Jean-Hubert Martin has pointed out, that Malevich was "seduced by the luminous qualities of white plaster and by the sharpness and purity which it restored to volume."[96] In fact, light serves the same function as colour, as demonstrated by the kinetic effects caused by changes in orientation and intensity of the source. In 1927 Malevich's main collaborator (work on the *Architektons* was based on group participation), Nikolai Suetin, noted that: "By lighting the suprematist volumetric form in one way or another, one can constantly see that light and shadow are present and show a certain interdependence."[97] By virtue of the sheer economy of means, it is not difficult to find a relationship between Malevich's *Architektons* and Minimal Art, which was to develop decades later.

There is a fundamental ambiguity present in the *Architektons:* are they sculptures or models for architecture? Although Malevich spoke of them as if they were sculptures, there is no doubt that he wanted them to be first and foremost architectonic works. He sometimes included tiny human figures in order to indicate the relative scale of the works, just as if they had been architect's models, but there are no openings for doors and windows in the *Architektons* (except for one opening in *Beta,* pl. 63) and the models were solid and not hollow as living quarters should be. Malevich defended himself from accusations that he had largely ignored the practical point of view by reminding his detractors that architecture should contribute to "the new construction of the utilitarian world."[98] He stated elsewhere that architecture, "apart from utilitarian solutions, also possesses a certain dynamic or static content, even an artistic-aesthetic content."[99] Feeling sheltered from criticism during his visit to the Dessau Bauhaus in 1927, Malevich gave more detailed information on his theories. The Polish writer Tadeusz Peiper left an interesting report of the meeting between Malevich and Walter Gropius, Principal of the Bauhaus:

Malevich differentiates between architecture and architectonics; the former has a utilitarian aim whereas the latter is strictly artistic. Architectonics produces work which only describes the artistic relationship of spatial forms; it does not take into consideration the fact that people will inhabit the form. . . . Gropius, who unlike the plastician Malevich is an architect by training, proposes another aim. For him, the method of construction depends with the greatest precision on the ultimate use of the building.[100]

Confronted with a real architect, Malevich emphasized the artistic aspects of architectonics, thus bringing them closer to sculpture than to architecture; in Russia his opponents were aware of this despite his denials and seized every suitable opportunity to criticize him. The *Architektons* nevertheless remain in the elegant words of

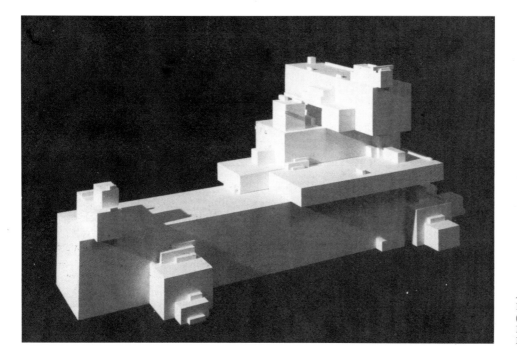

Alfa, 1923.
Plaster, 13 × 14⅝ × 33¼ in.
(33 × 37 × 84.5 cm).
Musée National d'Art
Moderne, Paris.

Andrei Nakov "formal proposals of a purely poetic order."[101] Unlike many architectural projects, they have not aged in the slightest.

In September 1923, four departments of plastic research were created at the Petrograd Fine Arts Museum and put under Malevich's supervision. The following year they were restructured to become the GINKhUK (the Petrograd State Institute of Painterly Culture). These official honours should not be taken to mean that Malevich's position was comfortable. His authoritarian character often led to confrontation with other museum officials and in the mid-1920s he expressed his resentment: "The Institute at Vitebsk has been forced to scuttle through insufficient funding; I came to Leningrad in the hope of building up a similar laboratory in the Academy of Arts, but all of my efforts have been shattered on the heads of the sphinxes who occupy posts there."[102] Even worse, many of the attacks were now coming from outside. Following Lenin's death, there was a marked tendency in all domains for a gradual return to tradition and an increasingly stronger opposition to all aspects of the avant-garde. Malevich was all too familiar with the conventional neo-classical style which pleased the country's leaders and he openly ridiculed it in his writings:

All of you, all of you revolutionary socialists without exception, you are in love with the styles of antiquity in the same way that women are in love with the hams of Apollo. Look at the monuments dedicated to the proletariat, there is no trace of the proletariat, it is the only Apollo which has remained under Minerva's helmet.[103]

These lines, published in 1923, reveal a profound awareness of what was to follow. But the conservative forces were not short of arguments; they even used the example of the Western "return to order" which had been growing in force since the end of World War I to support their theory and to throw back into the faces of the avant-garde. Radlov declared: "Picasso is painting naturalist canvases in the manner of Ingres. Carrà, Severini and the other Futurists are painting in the classical Italian manner."[104] This statement, in its Russian context, was full of implications.

Teapot, 1923. Porcelain, h. 7⅛ in. (18.2 cm). State Russian Museum, Leningrad.

The GINKhUK continued to pursue its various artistic and theoretical activities despite the opposition. Although Lissitzky had left for Germany, Chashnik, Suetin, Yudin and Ermolaeva were still the most active members and young blood like Pavel Mansurov had joined them. In 1923 a novel field of activity commenced when the Lomonosov Porcelain Factory requested their collaboration. Malevich designed a very original tea service along suprematist lines; he refused all symmetry and combined flat and curved surfaces with round and rectilinear forms. He also produced suprematist decorations for more standard items of crockery. At the time, officials were more aware than one would imagine of the originality of these suprematist creations and several were exhibited at the 1925 Exposition des Arts Décoratifs in Paris; indeed the suprematist tea sets were so successful that *L'Illustration* carried a photographic review of them in its 1st June 1925 issue. The GINKhUK team also created designs for printed fabrics and furniture and all other decorative arts.

SUPREMATISM CONTESTED

The privileged position of the Russian avant-garde suffered a serious threat in the latter half of the 1920s. Its most active opponents, the traditional painters, had grouped together under the banner of the Association of Russian Revolutionary Painters (AKhRR); their position strengthened through government support, and even though socialist realism was not yet the only official aesthetic movement accepted, they would finish by grouping together all the artists' associations in 1930. A number of conservative journalists raised their indignant voices against avant-garde research carried out at the expense of the State; they claimed it was not productive enough and was hardly accessible to the "people." It was in such a climate that Malevich was dismissed as director of the GINKhUK which was forced to close shortly after. This was a disturbing warning shot, but Malevich still

retained his band of faithful followers. Lunacharsky accepted his request for an artistic mission to the West. This was the only voyage Malevich ever made outside the Soviet Union and it was of capital significance. He took with him a considerable amount of material: canvases, graphic art, *Architektons,* several exercise books of writings and teaching charts to be used as visual aids; he also took several charts belonging to his friend and colleague Matiushin.

Malevich arrived in Poland to a triumphal welcome at the beginning of February 1927. The poet Tadeusz Peiper introduced the painter as a fellow countryman in his magazine *Zwrotnica*, undoubtedly because being of Polish descent he spoke the language fluently. Peiper had been informed of Malevich's visit by two past students of the Unovis at Vitebsk who were now resident in Poland, the painter Wladyslaw Strzeminski and the sculptor Katarzyna Kobro, both of whom worked in the suprematist manner. An exhibition of some thirty works by Malevich was held at Warsaw's Polonia Hotel for three weeks, and meetings and banquets followed in quick succession. Hostile to the constructivist movement which was gathering momentum, Malevich published "Deformation in Cubism" in *Zwrotnica,* attacking Constructivism and utilitarianism in art:

The true plastic artist will never examine objects according to their utilitarian value; on the contrary, all these utilitarian values will be subject to forms resulting from laws of plastic art. For example Constructivism is a current which has been preached by ex-plastic painters who only acknowledge utilitarian value now and dismiss art as a useless occupation.[105]

Although Tatlin, Malevich's old colleague at the GINKhUK, was not directly mentioned, the attack was aimed at him; at the time he was unaware of the interference to which Malevich had been subjected over the last months.

At the end of March, Malevich left for Germany accompanied by Peiper, who acted as his interpreter. In Germany he exhibited his works and gave a number of conferences and lectures. From Berlin he wrote to Matiushin: "I have demonstrated your tabulations along with my own. As to the interest at the demonstration of our work, one could not have wished for anything better."[106] Though he did not go to Paris, he visited the Bauhaus in Dessau where his reputation was already known thanks to Lissitzky. At the Bauhaus Malevich was reacquainted with Kandinsky and introduced to Walter Gropius, Mies van der Rohe, Hannes Meyer and Laszlo Moholy-Nagy, with whom he had some stimulating discussions on architecture, which was now a keen interest of his. Moholy-Nagy, converted to Suprematism by Lissitzky, supervised the publication of a summary of Malevich's writings on Suprematism and the "additional element in art" under the title of *Die gegenstandlose Welt* (*The Non-Objective World*) for the Bauhaus; it was the only book of Malevich's writings to be published abroad during his life, and despite its succinct and partial character, it was important for the diffusion of suprematist ideas outside the Soviet Union. On his return to Berlin, Malevich made new acquaintances, including Hans Arp and Kurt Schwitters, who were too distant from an aesthetic point of view for any lasting contact to have been established. The diatribe against Schwitters was predictable, as Suprematism was the antithesis of the German painter's "merz" collages and constructions founded on randomness and on a certain degree of sentimentalism which was very alien to Malevich. However, he was able to lay the foundations for a film on Suprematism with the film director Hans Richter; Malevich's simplified scenario has been conserved.

Germany had been particularly attentive to Malevich's work until the time of Hitler's rise to power. In 1920 Paul Westheim introduced Malevich as one of the great theorists of modern art in his book *Künstlerbekenntnisse;* similarly, Franz Seiwert and his friends always considered him to be an essential reference in their magazine *A bis Z* (1929-33).

An event which was to mark the destiny of Malevich's work took place during his visit to Berlin. The Berlin Association of Progressive Artists, to which his friends Hans von Riesen and Hugo Häring belonged, succeeded in organizing a solo exhibition of Malevich's work in the context of the Grosse Berliner Kunstausstellung. Malevich exhibited the important selection of works which he had brought with him at the exhibition which opened on 7th May and closed on 30th September. Meanwhile, Malevich decided to return to the Soviet Union (5th June) either because he had been called back or because he was worried about the increasing number of slanderous attacks being levelled against him in Russia. Hoping to return to Berlin in the not too distant future, he entrusted all his artistic effects, including his writings and his own and Matiushin's charts, to Hugo Häring. This act had two major consequences both for the artist and his future public.

Malevich was never able to recover the works which he had left in Germany and which in many cases represented milestones in his artistic development. It is not clear whether he believed them to be lost forever or abandoned to progressive decay. The fact is that for Malevich, who always insisted on showing the stages of his artistic development, these works were considered to be lost or inaccessible and this state of affairs was intolerable. It was then that he decided to paint copies of those lost works which had been executed at different stages of his career in order to conserve a testimony of the logical development of his work. This helps to explain why two versions of many of his paintings exist, and why the dating of his work is such a complicated and confusing task.

Fortunately, very little of what was left behind in Germany was lost. Häring carefully stored everything away and, despite the vicissitudes of German history, the hoard was discovered in 1951. Most of the works, excluding those which had been purchased by the Museum of Modern Art in New York after the Cubism and Abstract Art exhibition of 1936, were acquired by the Stedelijk Museum in Amsterdam in 1956. For many years this collection was the only source of information on Malevich's work because the U.S.S.R. had imposed a long period of silence on his avant-garde art.

When he returned from Berlin, Malevich worked at the State Institute for the History of Art in Leningrad. He continued to pursue his architectonic research with Chashnik and Suetin. Certain art historians believe that Malevich continued this line of research until around 1930, but it is probable that he continued to construct *Architektons* until well after that date and that they coexisted with his return to figurative art much later. A letter written on 29th September 1933 to the Director of the Russian Museum includes a request for material (plaster, wood and a source of water, etc.) as well as the assistance of photographic services in order to continue his "experimental work closely related to the theory of architecture."[107] But the art historians at the Leningrad Institute disputed Malevich's work so hotly and persistently that he was finally expelled in 1929 and was then reemployed by the Kiev Art Institute, where he worked for two and a half weeks per month.

Not all official institutions were completely unfavourable to Malevich, however, for in November 1929 a retrospective of his work was held at the State Tretyakov Gallery. As he wanted to show the logical internal development of the different stages of his work from Cubism to Alogism and then to Suprematism, he repainted the canvases which he held to be key works and which had been left behind in Germany; whenever he considered it necessary, he antedated canvases since, like for many avant-garde painters, it was of the utmost importance to him to prove that he had been the first to innovate or to experiment in certain fields. A large proportion of the works shown in Moscow were also shown the following year in Kiev, the city where he now occupied a new post and where, since most Moscow magazines rejected his collaboration, he regularly published articles in *Nova Generatsiya*.

THE RETURN TO PAINTING

After his *White on White* period, Malevich painted a few suprematist compositions, but devoted himself above all to pedagogy, writing and the *Architektons*. It is not clear whether he returned to painting suddenly or progressively; in any case, in order to prepare the 1929–30 retrospectives of his work he had to copy from memory a number of earlier paintings, either because they had been lost or had remained in Germany. For Malevich, who had fixed ideas on how his artistic development should be understood, it seemed logical that he should paint the missing links in his development retrospectively. Thus, while repainting earlier paintings in 1928 he took advantage of the opportunity to emphasize certain points or to modify dates to illustrate that he had been far more innovative than he really was. These acts must have forced him to reappraise painting in a concrete way, and it is probable that he rediscovered the pleasure of the paint brush and the canvas which he had forgotten. It is from this period that the so-called "return to painting" dates.

Even after the Cold War, the West often gloated when it thought it saw an about-turn or a "game of pretend" in Malevich's final style.[108] This appraisal of the situation, which is most probably of political inspiration, holds little truth when challenged with aesthetic reflection or with the history of art. Malevich was certainly not the type of person who would grovel to the régime or try to please the masters who held the official line in painting. Although he may have made some minor concessions (are the statues placed on some of the *Architektons* Malevich's own idea or his complying with external pressure?), they would never have led to the total surrender of his art. He did not "pretend" in order to survive, no more than Herbin did when he returned to figurative art in the 1920s; nobody forced him to return to figurative art any more than Jean Hélion was forced to return to figurative art in 1939. It is neither regression nor progression; it is an act which depends only on aesthetic choice.

In the case of Malevich and Tatlin, who had also returned to the easel and who painted some nudes and still-lifes around 1930, there was without any doubt a return to painting. The most genuine artists are concerned with not repeating themselves once they have exhausted a given line of research. Their art has led them to a point of no return as in the case of Malevich's *White on White* or Duchamp's ready-mades and the artist is faced with a silence, the end of his activity, but after a long period of careful thought he sees that it is possible to start afresh from this "zero level" where he has taken his art. Thus Duchamp from his silence secretly prepared his ultimate work, the great *Étant donnés* (*Given that*); similarly Malevich took up painting again from a totally different viewpoint. He did not resume figurative painting to come closer to the socialist realism of the official line of painters whom he did not frequent but, as Pontus Hulten wrote, because "the themes of his return to figurative art were more interior, more personal, even inherent to the evolution of his work."[109] There is no progress in art, and Malevich's new manner was neither more nor less progressive.

Malevich's late canvases were not generally dated, but a probable chronological order can be established. The first of the late canvases resemble works of the cubist period so closely (e.g. *Woodcutter* of 1911 and *Taking in the Rye* of 1912, pl. 15) that they have often been taken to be much earlier than they really are. If one considers *At the Dacha*, *Haymaking* or *Peasant in the Fields* (all from 1928–32) it will be seen that behind the tubular and conical structure of the bodies and limbs of the subjects, the rest of the painting is simply a composition of bright colours which lacks depth of field and where the half tones disappear. When applied to radically geometrical forms, it is the colour rather than the construction that dominates the canvas. *Peasant in the Fields* is an extreme example of this manner; the peasant is a stiff, symmetrical robot-like figure, a huge body surmounted by an absurdly small head with stylized features and a rectangular red and white beard. He stands out from a uniformly coloured bright blue sky and brightly coloured geometrical fields, while behind him a train is seen passing. Malevich also painted several half-length figures; *Head of a Peasant* (pl. 74) is divided into four red and white quarters, whereas the head of *Female Portrait* (pl. 88) is a regular oval of uniform white with oddly coloured stylized features. Both are equally inexpressive. Towards the end of the 1920s Malevich explained the metallic appearance of the characters which resemble those of 1912:

Provincial painterly culture attacks the metallic culture of the town and accuses it of being incomprehensible to the masses, whereas the plough is comprehensible to any peasant and small child, and the electric plough is incomprehensible to a whole village, being the fabulous monster it is.... Therefore, the painter is told that he must create such things which are comprehensible to the masses; the peasant would say: one must create a plough which is comprehensible to everybody.[110]

Perhaps the question lies in knowing whether the masses, if such an entity really exists, associated themselves more closely with those characters carved out of ploughs or with conventional painting. Remembering the preference for the drawings and the colours of the peasants of his childhood, who had not yet been affected by mass culture, Malevich was certain that his new works would be perfectly understood.

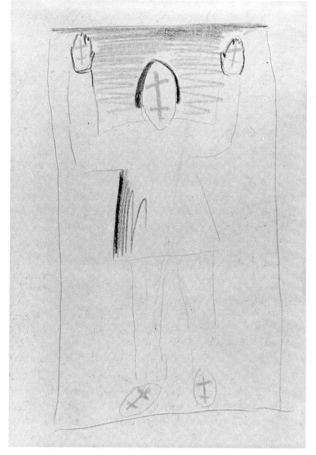

Woman with a Rake, 1928–32. Oil on canvas, 39⅜×29½ in. (100×75 cm). State Tretyakov Gallery, Moscow.

Standing Figure, c. 1930. Colour crayons, 14⅜×8⅞ in. (36.5×22.5 cm). Stedelijk Museum, Amsterdam.

What meaning should be given to the paintings depicting countryside scenes? Valentine Marcadé assumes that they illustrated the helplessness of the bewildered peasants faced with the mechanization and collectivization to which they were brutally subjected at the time.[111] This would explain the train behind the peasant in *Peasant in the Fields* and the tiny aeroplanes in the sky in *Head of a Peasant:* machines were taking away the peasant's freedom and his traditional agricultural methods. There is probably some truth in this, because when Malevich was writing his autobiography in which he expressed his love for the traditional world of the peasant, the inhabitants of the countryside were being brutally pushed into line and massacred if they resisted the edicts of the five-year plan. The absence of arms in *Peasant and Horse* (1933) and other works (pl. 79, 80) has been interpreted as a sign of mutilation and the featureless faces of some characters as the denial of personality, but caution should always be exercised to avoid too tendentious an interpretation being made; could the same be said of the faceless and armless characters in the paintings of Giorgio de Chirico and Albert Savinio from 1914 onwards? The faceless man (pl. 81) with the body of a mannequin or of a robot has been widely represented, after his initial appearance in metaphysical and futurist painting, by artists such as Wyndham Lewis in England, Ivo Pannaggi in Italy, George Grosz and Oskar Schlemmer in Germany, Sandor Bortnyik in Hungary, the Belgian René Magritte and even Max Ernst. The faceless man is present in all modern movements because of the diversity of interpretations which he can be given. The fact that he has been used widely and even within Malevich's own circle

of followers, by Suetin to decorate the *Baby* set of porcelain, invites even greater caution when offering an interpretation.[112]

In the second stage of his return to painting, Malevich only painted half- or full-length figures: peasants, Moujiks sporting orthodox beards (pl. 77) and sportsmen clad in bright colours (pl. 81). In all cases the faces are blank, flat and without the slightest feature; sometimes they are completely black (pl. 78, 80), the only exceptions being two of a group of three *Bathers* (pl. 93). The numerous preparatory drawings and sketches for paintings which may or may not have been executed do not include any more facial features, as in fact was the case with the masks designed for the characters in *Victory over the Sun.* If they sometimes wear a sign (a cross, a sickle or a hammer, e.g. pl. 94, 95), this only reinforces their anonymity. Malevich has at most given his men a beard, which is deliberately hanging off the face (pl. 96). The carefully drawn men and women stand out from a uniform and luminous sky and a flat landscape of candy-stripe colour where an occasional house or two is sometimes positioned (pl. 83, 84, 85). The houses are as impenetrable as the featureless faces, because they have no doors or windows; sometimes the houses replace human figures and are the only figurative elements on the canvas. The calm beauty and the gay colours of works like *Woman with a Rake, Three Female Figures* (pl. 80) or *Landscape with Five Houses* (1928–32) are striking, they are fascinating but without pathos. One cannot avoid a certain uneasy feeling when confronted with *Complex Presentiment: Half-Figure in a Yellow Shirt* (pl. 77), in which a man with a featureless, oval face wearing a yellow shirt (Mayakovsky used to wear a similar garment in the days of Futurism to shock the public) stands immobile in front of a clearly visible house with red walls and no openings set in a very simplified landscape of four coloured bands and a sky. If an attempt is made to attribute some meaning to these works on top of their formal beauty, a form of Surrealism could be invoked, as Pontus Hulten does in the introduction to the *Malévitch: Architectones* catalogue, or of social protest as we have seen above. But did Malevich have Realism, Surrealism or Humanism in mind when he painted these works? I very much doubt it. Did he ever say that he was abandoning the ethical position of Suprematism? Bearing in mind the strict economy of Malevich's work, Emmanuel Martineau's interpretation is far more convincing:

The question is no longer the alternative between abstraction and figuration; the question is that Suprematism emphasized a certain image, and that image was initially an image of the world and it must now become an image of man, hence Malevich's stubbornness, a positive quality, during many years when he ceaselessly drew the image of man, the new face of man on small pieces of paper.[113]

The image of man was in fact the major preoccupation of the new Suprematism. In all cases, the more or less pessimistic socio-political interpretations of Malevich's armless and faceless characters should be used with extreme caution. To illustrate the point it is worth remembering that several years earlier Matisse, who was not in the least preoccupied with human tragedy, had also painted faceless figures and truncated limbs (e.g. in the large *Bathers by a Stream* of 1910-17). Also worthy of mention is the fact that new figurative Suprematism had a wide following and that several of Malevich's disciples, notably Anna Leporskaya and K. N. Rojdestvensky, painted works where characters with oval faces stand out from backgrounds of brightly coloured stripes and peasants with very vaguely drawn features sport beards which are barely attached to their faces. If these images were ugly, Suetin would not have used faceless peasants for the decoration of the dinner services designed for the Lomonosov Potteries around 1930. Malevich's work is always complex and cannot readily avoid all ambiguity.

During the third stage of Malevich's return to painting, probably around 1931-32, he refused the conventionalism of his characters and introduced a notion of movement; the absence of arms in *Peasants* and *Peasant and Horse* is particularly surprising and gave way to some speculation. At the same time, the technique of the paintings changed: the contours lost their sharp edges, the brush strokes became more expressionistic or hurried, the thickness of the paint was uneven and sometimes allowed the bare canvas to show through. In the autumn of 1931 Malevich wrote to the Ukrainian painter Lev Kramarenko: "I am thinking of undertaking some painting, of doing some symbolic pictures. I am trying to produce an image."[114] This revelation suggests that Malevich was undergoing a crisis, and that he was working in doubt and by fits and starts. But what exactly did he mean by "symbolic"? Symbolism can be misleading as in the famous canvas *Red Cavalry* (pl. 82), shown for the first time in 1932, where three squadrons of red horsemen ride across a distant horizon which is rendered immense by the luminous sky and the coloured bands

representing the earth. The revolutionary symbolism is so blatant that, at the time when Malevich was considered to be anti-Soviet, there were people who affirmed that the painter had been obliged to add figures to testify to the glory of the Revolution. The beauty and the coherence of the painting should have rendered such a thought unimaginable and the preparatory drawings leave no doubt as to the central role which the horsemen should play.[115] The symbolism is far more difficult to decipher in a work like *Running Man* (pl. 96), where symbols abound. A man depicted in full flight seems to be fleeing the objects present in the background; on the right, a red and a white house separated by a bloody sword which perhaps represents the reason of the State, and on the left, a large cross with a blackened base which appears to be rotting. Possible interpretations come to mind and it is not necessary to dwell on them any longer than it would be desirable to dwell on the possible symbolism of the colours red and white. The character is definitely a peasant, instantly recognizable by his costume and his beard; he is fleeing from the sword and the cross, but why is his skin black? And why has one of his hands been painted over? These questions, together with many others, remain unanswered in the absence of documentary evidence and adequate study of this type of work.

If the works of this period pose so many problems of interpretation, it may be because Malevich's career was also full of confusion and contradictions; we have before us an artist who had just enjoyed a retrospective at the State Tretyakov Gallery, who had been commissioned to paint a mural for the Red Theatre, Leningrad, and who, in 1930, was detained by the police and held for several days for questioning on suspicion of having subversive ideas. There were fears for his freedom but he was allowed to return to his occupations; seven or eight years later, under the increasingly hard line of the Stalinist régime, he would not have been dealt with so leniently. In 1931, he executed the mural for the Red Theatre. In 1932, he was given a post at the Research Laboratory of the Leningrad State Russian Museum, which he held for the rest of his life. His work appeared at official exhibitions; he exhibited a wide selection of his work at the Artists of the RSFSR over a Period of 15 Years exhibition in Leningrad (November 1932 to May 1933). Bearing in mind the atmosphere of suspicion surrounding avant-garde art and his police custody, it is surprising to see such a wide cross-section of his work of the previous fifteen years. Photographs of the exhibition show he exhibited suprematist paintings, including *Black Square*, and more recent works like *Red House* (pl. 85), *Three Female Figures* (pl. 80), *Peasant*, several objects and an important number of *Architektons*.

The spectacular presence of Malevich in an official exhibition did not in any way reflect the general opinion of Soviet art. Igor Grabar, the painter and critic who was on excellent terms with the régime, explained in his exhibition catalogue that this type of art was necessary in order to "purify" painting and to allow the coming of Socialist Realism, but that it was obsolete from the moment the slogan "back towards realism, forward towards the masses" had been coined.[116]

What were the reasons for the change in Malevich's art? Had he been influenced by the wave of Socialist Realism, including the work of old radicals like Tatlin, which had swept over Soviet art? Did he too want to try it out? Was he tired of repeating faceless figures indefinitely? Whatever the reasons, Malevich's art changed direction around 1932, although the human figure continued to feature in it. *Girl with Comb in Hair* (1932–33, pl. 98) retains the dominant colours which marked the painter's return to painting; the girl's body and hair are geometrically constructed, but more detailed facial features enter into the design. With receding geometry and a more expressive figure, the portrait loses the impersonal touch which had characterized the previous portraits; this is true of *Girl with a Red Pole* (1932–33, pl. 99) where the girl's Pierrot-like features make the colour of her costume stand out remarkably. This marked the last step toward real portraits. Malevich painted several very conventional portraits; there are still some traces of his earlier works in the way the costume of *Female Worker* (1933, pl. 103) is handled, but his hand is hardly recognizable in the very ordinary looking *Portrait of V. A. Pavlov* (1933). The portraits can, however be very endearing when the artist paints somebody very close to him; *Portrait of Una* (1932–33, pl. 102), is a delightful half-figure portrait of the artist's twelve-year-old daughter in a garden.

The painter returned to a more realist style in the works of 1932–33, but only to relative Realism; the surprising *Girl with Comb in Hair* (pl. 98) is closer to the science-fiction of the film *Aelita* (1924) than to Realism, and her clothing is even more revolutionary than the suprematist costumes which Malevich had drawn in 1923. The painter was not only obeying an interior urge but also a contemporary tendency which was very distant from Socialist Realism, in which even Tatlin and Rodchenko had participated; it was a tendency which had already brought back several painters like Severini and Herbin to figurative painting; as for Picasso, he changed radically from one manner to another at will, moving from abstraction to realism and back again as and when he wished.

It was in his last paintings that the painter, who now significantly signed his canvases with a black square, rediscovered his power to surprise. His inspiration was now to be found in the painters of the Renaissance, as

Malevich at work. Leningrad, 3 April 1933.

Portrait of the Artist's Wife (pl. 101) or *Male Portrait (N. N. Punin?)* (1933) reveal. The figures, dressed in suprematist clothing of bright and bold colours, were painted in profile against dark backgrounds in the traditional pose of renaissance portraits; the photographic realism of the faces contrasts with the somewhat surprising geometrical effect of the clothes. Malevich's last masterpiece was his *Self-Portrait* (pl. 106), which was finished when he had only a few months to live. There is a vivid contrast between this self-portrait and those painted during his early days; his reference is not Fauvism or Cubism but the timeless Renaissance: the artist has even portrayed himself wearing clothes which resemble those of many renaissance subjects. But there is no nostalgia as when de Chirico portrays himself in classical or Veronese surroundings in seventeenth-century costume with his sword beside him. Unlike most of the other portraits, Malevich painted himself against a pale background and without background details or accessories. He is standing immortally in front of eternity with an open hand as if he were offering something coming from himself, his life and his work, thirty years of painting. In the bottom right-hand corner there is a final reminder of his revolution: the Black Square.

DEATH AND TRANSFIGURATION

The years from 1928 to 1932 marked a turning point, the old realist tendencies, inherited from the Wanderers of the nineteenth century and favoured by the country's leaders, returned with force with the Association of Artists of Revolutionary Russia (AKhRR), which became increasingly powerful as it progressively imposed the idea of proletarian art as the only valid form of art. Andrei Zhdanov and Igor Grabar loudly and hollowly celebrated Socialist Realism in the name of the artists at the Congress of the Writer's Union in 1934. Malevich was not called into question. In April 1935, shortly before his death, he featured at the First Exhibition of Leningrad Painters, no doubt because the policy of proletarian realism was not yet sufficiently well organized, but also because of his historical importance and the huge respect so many painters had for him.

During the last months of his incurable illness, Malevich was unable to work. The last photographs taken show him on his sickbed with a tired, drawn face and long hair and beard resembling that of the peasants he so loved. On the walls around him are his last portraits, his faceless figures, his suprematist abstractions and at the centre of everything his *Black Square,* proof, if it were needed, that for him and his friends the value of his old and new works was equal. Malevich never changed style except of his own free will; he was one of those men who preferred to die rather than to betray his work, like Isaac Babel and Boris Pilniak and thousands of others who died at the hands of Stalinist intolerance in the following years. To suggest that he could have agreed to prostitute his art to the régime would be to insult his memory. All his work obeyed his own laws; his last *Self-Portrait*, like *Black*

Square, was a refusal to comply with the edicts of Socialist Realism which for some years had covered, and for a good many decades would cover, walls with brave soldiers, joyful labourers, tractors reaping rich harvests, mothers with large families, and huge effigies of Stalin. Malevich never contributed to this paraphernalia and there is no reason to believe that he would have done so had he lived longer.

When Malevich died on 15th May 1935, his followers were distressed. Conscious of the great loss, they photographed him lying in state on his bed or in his coffin surrounded by his works; his coffin was adorned with the suprematist circle and square painted by Suetin. It was the State Russian Museum which took possession of most of the works which Malevich had kept up to his death. Photographs bear testimony to the size of the huge crowds which came to the funeral; the cortège drove up the Nevski Prospect under the eyes of onlookers, mourners carried flowers and a lorry decorated with *Black Square* carried the coffin. This last *Black Square* was placed on his tomb at Nemchinovska. It has been observed that this ceremony which attracted such a crowd was a form of silent protest against the régime. It is probably true that the fact that this unorthodox painter who was not accepted by officialdom was nevertheless represented at the most important exhibitions conferred on him a special aura.

After Malevich's death, a leaden veil of silence fell over his work in the U.S.S.R. and it was confined to stock rooms in museums. In the West, for twenty years the small number of works on show could not give the slightest impression of the magnitude of his oeuvre, despite the enthusiasm shown by artists like Moholy-Nagy, Strzeminsky and Kobo or Sophie Taeuber's magazine *Plastique,* which rendered Malevich a visually striking homage in its first issue (Paris, 1937).

The 1950s saw the veil being lifted; the works entrusted to Hugo Häring in 1927 had come to light and were acquired by the Stedelijk Museum which became the Mecca of modern painting. It would still take a number of years before the U.S.S.R. would lift its prohibition on abstract art and Malevich's work in particular and agree to release works for important exhibitions at home and abroad. The first paintings to be released resurfaced in the U.S.S.R. in 1962; other public showings followed, notably the one-man exhibition of 1978 and Paris-Moscow Exhibition at the Centre Georges Pompidou, Paris, which followed shortly; at last the West could see the painter's major works which had been kept under a bushel for more than forty years.

But this long silence does not mean that Malevich did not have any followers after his death. In the Soviet Union, Lissitzky and Suetin introduced Malevich's suprematist principles into their fields of applied and decorative arts wherever possible. Obviously, what was known of Malevich's work could not be used as a serious reference for the world until the 1950s, partly due to the fact that he was advanced for his time but also because of the difficulties in gaining access to the work. After the 1950s, his work aroused a growing interest. Artists as different as Vasarely and Yves Klein claimed *Black Square* to be a seminal influence for them because of its intransigent geometry and pure monochrome colour. The homages paid to this canvas include an aquatint by Dan Flavin (1988), an easel painting by Marcelle Cahn (1966) and a monumental work by Vasarely at the University of Caracas (1954), and, of course, Jean Tinguely's *Méta-Malévitch* (1954) mobile reliefs. Similarly, Sol Le Witt and many other American artists of the 1960s and 1970s have acknowledged their debt to Malevich. Though a bewilderingly wide range of artists salute Malevich or claim to be his followers, a certain category of journalists have taken over Malevich to turn him into the art world's counterpart of the poet Mandelstam, a martyr of Stalinism. This fictional legend is inaccurate in the case of Malevich, as he did not experience any more isolation than Kupka, nor was he poorer than Mondrian or Herbin in the 1920s and 1930s. All of the major pioneers of abstraction had experienced an extremely difficult career, whether they were ignored by the official aesthetic line or confronted with the indifference of the general public and the art loving world. It would be an error to assume that instant recognition or wealth would have made any significant contribution to their work. Obviously, it is regrettable that their living conditions were so harsh, but what matters today is the quality of their art and not the number of medals or awards they might have been awarded. When artists are sure of their theory, they do not need official approval.

Malevich was convinced that his aesthetic values were right; he was without doubt a very demanding and authoritarian master, but to see in this an all-excluding totalitarian movement like the Socialist Realism of the hard Stalinist years would be a profound mistake. Those who have written on Malevich have never held the divine truth. We should beware of the history of art which claims to be objective but which is the child of its time. We should beware of approximate reproductions or bad copies which detract from the original. Whenever possible, we should examine the original works themselves. Incidentally, the square is not really square and the black is not really black.

Montgeron, November 1989.

Note

This book was on press when Jean-Claude Marcadé's *Malévitch* appeared in the autumn of 1990 (Paris, Editions Casterman). I regret not being able to make reference to it here not only because it goes without saying that Jean-Claude Marcadé is one of the most eminent specialists on Malevich, but also because he kindly lent me the proofs of his translations of some hitherto unpublished material by Malevich. There is little to be said about the proceedings of the recent *Malévitch* congress (Flammarion, 1990), which reproduces all the errors of the catalogue of the international exhibition, "Kazimir Malevich, 1878-1935" (1989).

On reading the proofs of this book in December 1990, I realize that I was a bad prophet. Malevich is still being used as a political pawn; the catalogue of the modified version of the international exhibition now being held in Washington is prefaced by two texts signed respectively by the presidents of the United States and the Soviet Union.

NOTES

Most of the original French quotations of Malevich's writings are taken from J.C. Marcadé's four-volume translation of the painter's writings, *Écrits*, vols I, II, III (forthcoming) and IV. Whenever possible, the English translations are taken from established English editions of Malevich's writings (notably T. Andersen) and the English source acknowledged. Where this has not been possible, the translation has been made from the French source.

1. J.C. Marcadé (ed.), *Malévitch, 1875-1935: Actes du colloque international tenu au Centre Pompidou, Musée National d'Art Moderne, les 4 et 5 mai 1978,* Lausanne, 1979, p. 153.

2. *Ibid., loc. cit.*

3. *Ibid.,* p. 155.

4. *Ibid.,* pp. 154–56.

5. *Ibid.,* p. 161.

6. K.S. Malevich, "1/42 Notes," *Essays on Art, 1915-1933,* ed. Troels Andersen, trans. Xenia Glowacki-Prus and Arnold McMillin, London, Rapp and Whiting, 1969, vol. II, p. 154.

7. J.C. Marcadé (ed.), *op. cit.,* p. 167.

8. L. Zhadova, *Malevich: Suprematism and Revolution in Russian Art, 1910-1930,* trans. Alexander Lieven, London, Thames & Hudson, 1982, p. 12.

9. K.S. Malevich, "An Attempt to Determine the Relation Between Colour and Form in Painting," *op. cit.,* vol. I, p. 133.

10. K.S. Malevich, "An Analysis of New and Imitative Art (Paul Cézanne)," *ibid.,* vol. II, p. 22.

11. J.C. Marcadé (ed.), *op. cit.,* p. 163.

12. *Ibid.,* p. 168.

13. Suetin's comments appear in the annexes of J.C. Marcadé's French translation of Malevich's work, K.S. Malévitch, *Ecrits II: Le miroir suprématiste,* Lausanne, L'Age d'Homme, 1977, p. 179.

14. Quoted in J.C. Marcadé (ed.), *op. cit.,* p. 108.

15. L. Zhadova, *op. cit.,* p. 14.

16. M. Pleynet, *Painting and System,* trans. S.N. Godfrey, Chicago, University of Chicago Press, 1984, p. 138.

17. K.S. Malevich, "On New Systems in Art," *op. cit.,* vol. I, pp. 90–91. The essay was revised the following year and published under the more explicit title of *De Cézanne au suprématisme* (*cf.* K.S. Malévitch, *Écrits I: De Cézanne au suprématisme,* trans. J.C. Marcadé, Lausanne, L'Age d'Homme, 1974, pp. 75–116).

18. *Ibid.,* vol. I, p. 94.

19. "Léger, Gris, Herbin, Metzinger," *ibid.,* vol. II, pp. 66–67.

20. Quoted in V. Markov, *Russian Futurism: A History,* Berkeley, University of California, 1968, p. 46.

21. "Rayonnists and Futurists: A Manifesto" (1913), quoted in J.E. Bowlt (ed.), *Russian Art of the Avant-Garde: Theory and Criticism, 1902-1934,* New York, 1976, p. 90.

22. B. Livshits, *The One and a Half-Eyed Archer,* trans., introduced and annotated by J.E. Bowlt, Newton (Mass.), Oriental Research Partners, 1977, p. 210.

23. K.S. Malevich, "On New Systems in Art," *op. cit.,* vol. I, p. 102.

24. *Ibid.,* vol. I, pp. 96–97.

25. K.S. Malévitch, "Du cubisme au suprématisme," *Écrits I,* p. 38.

26. Quoted in J.E. Bowlt, *op. cit.,* p. 134.

27. K.S. Malevich, "An Attempt to Determine the Relation between Colour and Form in Painting," *op. cit.,* vol. II, pp. 145–46.

28. Matiushin quoting Ouspensky in "Du Cubisme," *Cahiers du M.N.A.M.,* no. 2, Paris, 1979, p. 290. English translation from P.D. Ouspensky, *Tertium Organum. The Third Canon of Thought. A Key to the Enigmas of the World,* rev. trans. by E. Kadloubovsky and the author, London, Routledge and Kegan Paul, 1981, p. 17 and p. 133.

29. From "La tournée de Marinetti en Russie" in K.S. Malévitch, *Écrits II,* p. 145.

30. *Sofia,* No. 8, Moscow, 1914.

31. K.S. Malévitch, "Premier congrès pan-russe des bardistes de l'avenir (poètes futuristes)," *Écrits II,* p. 41.

32. B. Livshits, *op. cit.,* p. 164.

33. K.S. Malevich, "On New Systems in Art," *op. cit.,* vol. I, p. 118.

34. The quotations from *Victory over the Sun* are taken from the translation by Ewa Bartos and Victoria Nes Kirby, *The Drama Review,* vol. 15, no. 4, 1971.

35. Letter dated 27 May 1915 to Matiushin in J.C. Marcadé (ed.), *op. cit.,* p. 181.

36. K.S. Malévitch, "On New Systems in Art," *op. cit.,* vol. I, p. 95.

37. K.S. Malévitch, "Du cubisme et du futurisme. Le nouveau réalisme pictural," *Écrits I,* ed. cit., p. 65.

38. K.S. Malevich, "Secret Vices of the Academicians," *op. cit.,* vol. I, pp. 17–18.

39. K.S. Malévitch, "On New Systems in Art," *op. cit.,* vol. I, p. 96.

40. K.S. Malévitch, "Painting and the Problem of Architecture," *op. cit.,* vol. II, p. 15.

41. Quoted in V. Markov, *op. cit.,* pp. 130–31.

42. "Artists of the World! A Written Language for Planet Earth: A Common System of Hieroglyphs for the People of our Planet," in V. Khlebnikov, *Collected Works of Velimir Khlebnikov. I. Letters and Theoretical Writings,* trans. Paul Schmidt, ed. Charlotte Douglas, Cambridge (Mass.), Harvard University Press, 1987, p. 367.

43. V. Markov, *op. cit.,* p. 80.

44. *Ibidem.*

45. K.S. Malévitch, "Du cubisme au suprématisme. Le nouveau réalisme pictural," *Écrits I,* p. 43.

46. J.C. Marcadé (ed.), *op. cit.,* p. 14.

47. K.S. Malevich, "On New Systems in Art," *op. cit.,* vol. I, p. 99.

48. K.S. Malévitch, "Du cubisme au Suprématisme," *Écrits I,* p. 38.

49. *Ibid.,* p. 39.

50. *Ibid.,* p. 38.

51. V. Kandinsky, *Concerning the Spiritual in Art,* trans. and introd. M.T.H. Sadler, New York, Dover, 1977, p. 47.

52. K.S. Malevich, "Non-Objective Creation and Suprematism," *op. cit.,* vol. I, p. 120.

53. K.S. Malevich, "Non-Objectivity," *The World as Non-Objectivity. Unpublished Writings 1922-1925,* ed. Troels Andersen, trans. Xenia Glowacki-Prus and Edmund T. Little, Copenhagen, Borgen, 1976, p. 91.

54. J.C. Marcadé (ed.), *op. cit.,* p. 182; also quoted in L. Zhadova, *op. cit.,* p. 123.

55. B. Lopatine, "Extraits de la presse à propos de l'exposition 0.10," in K.S. Malévitch, *Écrits II,* p. 153.

56. K.S. Malevich, "Letter to Alexandre Benois," *Essays on Art. 1915-1933,* vol. I, p. 47.

57. V. Khlebnikov, "Excerpt from the Tables of Destiny," *op. cit.,* vol. I, p. 419.

58. K.S. Malevich, *ibid.,* p. 45.

59. P.D. Ouspensky, *op. cit.,* p. 245.

60. K.S. Malevich, "Non-Objectivity," *The World as Non-Objectivity. Unpublished Writings 1922-1925,* p. 145.

61. El Lissitzky, *Life, Letters, Texts,* introd. H. Read and Sophie Lissitzky-Küppers, London, Thames & Hudson, 1980, pp. 337–38.

62. *C.f. Cercle et Carré*, No. 2, April 1930.

63. K.S. Malévitch, "L'axe de la couleur et du volume," *Écrits II*, p. 73.

64. Quoted in K.S. Malévitch, *ibid.*, p. 179 (see note 13, above).

65. Vasarely, *Plasticien*, 1979, p. 177.

66. Quoted in L. Zhadova, *op. cit.*, p. 122.

67. K.S. Malevich, "On Poetry," *Essays on Art. 1915-1933*, vol. I, p. 81.

68. "Space in Painting and Suprematism," quoted in L. Zhadova, *op. cit.*, p. 326.

69. K.S. Malevich, "The Problems of Art and the Role of its Supressors," *op. cit.*, vol. I, p. 49.

70. K.S. Malevich, "The Question of Imitative Art," *ibid.*, vol. I, p. 170.

71. *Ibid.*, vol. I, p. 167.

72. *Ibid.*, vol. I, p. 168.

73. "On New Systems in Art," *ibid.*, vol. I, p. 107.

74. "The Question of Imitative Art," *ibid.*, vol. I, p. 166.

75. See S. Fauchereau, *L'Avant-Garde Russe*, Paris, Belfond, 1979.

76. K.S. Malevich, "On New Systems in Art," *op. cit.*, vol. I, p. 103.

77. *Ibid.*, p. 95.

78. *Ibid.*, p. 102.

79. K. S. Malevich, "Suprematism: 34 Drawings," *op. cit.*, vol. I, p. 123.

80. *Ibid.*, vol. I, p. 122.

81. N. Punin, "About New Art Groupings," quoted in K.S. Malévitch, *Écrits II*, p. 167. Translation from L. Zhadova, *op. cit.*, p. 322.

82. K.S. Malevich, "Suprematism: 34 Drawings," *op. cit.*, vol. I, pp. 127-28.

83. L. Robel, *Manifestes Futuristes Russes*, Paris, Les Éditeurs Fran-çais Réunis, 1971, p. 59.

84. K.S. Malevich, "Architecture as a Slap in the Face to Ferro-Concrete," *op. cit.*, vol. I, p. 64.

85. K.S. Malevich, "Suprematism: 34 Drawings," *ibid.*, vol. I, p. 128.

86. J.E. Bowlt (ed.), *Russian Art of the Avant-Garde. (Theory and Criticism) 1902-1934*, p. 153.

87. K.S. Malevich, "The Question of Imitative Art," *op. cit.*, vol. I, p. 173.

88. *Ibid.*, vol. I, p. 172.

89. K.S. Malevich, "UNOVIS - the Champions of New Art," quoted in L. Zhadova, *op. cit.*, p. 299.

90. J.C. Marcadé (ed.), *op. cit.*, p. 85.

91. K.S. Malévitch, "L'architecture, la peinture de chevalet et la sculpture," *Écrits III, Izologia*, trans. J.C. and V. Marcadé, (forthcoming).

92. L. Zhadova, *op. cit.*, p. 98; also included in the exhibition catalogue *Malévitch: Architectones*, Paris, Centre Pompidou, 1980, p. 22.

93. K.S. Malevich, "Painting and the Problem of Architecture," *Essays on Art, 1915-1933*, vol. II, p. 16.

94. J.H. Martin, "L'art suprématiste de la volumo-construction" in *Malévitch: Architectones*, p. 17.

95. *C.f.* C. Cooke's translation of Malevich, "Form, Colour and Space," *Art and Design*, vol. V, no. 5-6, 1989, pp. 45-47.

96. J.H. Martin, *op. cit.*, p. 18.

97. N. Suetin, notes on Unovis in K.S. Malévitch, *Écrits II*, p. 178.

98. K.S. Malévitch, "L'Ounovis," *ibid.*, p. 91.

99. K.S. Malévitch, "L'architecture, la peinture de chevalet et la sculpture," *Écrits III, Izologia*.

100. *Cahiers du M.N.A.M.*, no. 3, Centre Pompidou, 1980, p. 126.

101. A. Nakov, *Abstrait/Concret: Art non-objectif russe et polonais*, Paris, Transédition, 1981, p. 63.

102. K.S. Malévitch, *Écrits IV*, p. 132.

103. K.S. Malévitch, "Le poussah," *ibid.*, p. 99.

104. N. Radlov, "Vers les sources de l'art" in K.S. Malévitch, *ibid.*, p. 181.

105. *Cahiers du M.N.A.M.*, no. 2, Centre Pompidou, 1979, p. 314.

106. L. Zhadova, *op. cit.*, p. 125.

107. "Lettre au directeur du département artistique du Musée russe d'état" in *Malévitch: Architectones*, p. 43.

108. *C.f.* J. Ohayon, "Malévitch. Le degré zéro de l'architecture," *ibid.*, p. 25.

109. P. Hulten, introduction to *ibid.*, p. 7.

110. K.S. Malevich, "An Introduction to the Theory of the Additional Element in Painting," *The World as Non-Objectivity: Unpublished Writings, 1922-1925*, p. 194.

111. *Cahier Malévich*, Lausanne, 1983, p. 12.

112. *C.f.* L. Zhadova, *op. cit.*, figs. 260-63.

113. J.C. Marcadé (ed.), *op. cit.*, p. 109.

114. L. Zhadova, *op. cit.*, p. 114.

115. *C.f. Malévitch* exhibition catalogue, Paris, 1978, p. 76.

116. I. Grabar, "Une fête des maîtres du pinceau, du crayon et du burin," in K.S. Malévitch, *Écrits II*, p. 190.

CHRONOLOGY

1878–1895 Kazimir Severinovich Malevich, of Polish descent, born 11th February 1878 to Severin Antonovich (1845-1902) and Liudviga Alexandrovna (1858-1942) in Kiev (Ukraine). His father works in several sugar refineries in the environs of Kiev, at Parkhomovka and Volchok in particular. Malevich later revealed the importance of having grown up in the country. He paints his first painting at Konotop near Volchok and decides to become a painter. Meets the future composer Nikolai Roslavets. Is admitted to the Kiev School of Art.

1896 The family settles in Kursk. The young painter discovers the work (in reproduction) of the naturalist painters, the Wanderers. He paints from nature in the company of other amateur painters like Lev Kvachevsky, and organizes a small circle of artists. He feels that it would very important for his work to go to the great cultural centres of Moscow or St. Petersburg. Employed as technical draughtsman for the Kursk-Moscow railway company; saves in order to move to Moscow.

1901 Marries Kazimira Ivanova Zgleitz. The marriage would be short-lived.

1904 Finally arrives in Moscow. Malevich wants to enter the Moscow College of Painting, Sculpture and Architecture.

1905 Back in Kursk for a few months, he paints in the open air in neo-impressionist style. Mans the barricades of the December Revolution in Moscow.

1906 Malevich begins working in Fedor Rerberg's Moscow studio while regularly returning to Kursk.

1907 Earliest known mention of Malevich's name in a catalogue, alongside the names of Vladimir Burliuk, Alexandre Chevchenko, Natalia Goncharova, Vasily Kandinsky, Mikhail Larionov, Alexis Morgunov at the Moscow Association of Artists exhibition. He is impressed by the Blue Rose and the Wreath exhibitions.

1908 His *Studies for a Fresco* are exhibited at the Moscow Association of Artists exhibition. First Golden Fleece exhibition, which includes numerous contemporary Parisian artists. Malevich does not exhibit.

1909 Second Golden Fleece exhibition shows works by the Paris Fauves and Braque's *Grand nu,* first cubist work to enter the country. Marries Sofiya Mikhailovna Rafalovich.

1910 Exhibits *Bathing Woman* and other works at the first Knave of Diamonds exhibition, organized by Larionov and Goncharova. Meets Alexandra Exter and Varvara Stepanova at the show.

1911 Exhibits at the St. Petersburg Union of Youth exhibition together with other Moscow artists (David and Vladimir Burliuk, Goncharova, Larionov and Tatlin). Begins his neo-primitivist phase. Matisse travels to Moscow in the autumn to install *Dance* and *Music* in Shchukin's palace.

1912 Larionov and Goncharova withdraw from the Knave of Diamonds group, which has become too westernized for their taste, and found the Donkey's Tail which organizes its own exhibition where Malevich, Chagall, Chevchenko, Stepanova and Tatlin exhibit. Kandinsky invites Malevich to participate at the Blaue Reiter exhibition in Munich; he sends the primitivist *Head of a Peasant Girl.* Meets Mikhail Matiushin. Exhibits some primitivist works at the new Union of Youth exhibition, St. Petersburg. David Burliuk, Alexei Kruchenykh, Velimir Khlebnikov and Vladimir Mayakovsky publish the first Russian Futurist Manifesto, *A Slap in the Face of Public Taste,* in December. Malevich moves away from Larionov and draws closer to the Futurists, declaring himself Cubo-Futurist.

1913 Malevich enrolls in the Union of Youth movement. Cubo-futurist paintings (*The Knife Grinder*). Spends the summer at Matiushin's *dacha* in Uusikirkko (Finland). Publishes a futurist manifesto with Matiushin and Kruchenykh, and works with them on the opera *Victory over the Sun,* which is performed on 3rd and 5th December at the Luna Park Theatre, St. Petersburg. Malevich designs the costumes and set, Matiushin writes the music for Kruchenykh's libretto and Khlebnikov writes the foreword. Exhibits his cubo-futurist works for the last time at the Union of Youth exhibition with his first transrational or alogist works. Publication of *Three* (texts by Khlebnikov, Kruchenykh and the recently deceased Elena Guro, illustrations by Malevich). Begins to frequent Filonov, for whom he has the highest regard.

1914 Malevich participates in certain futurist events. Exhibits three cubo-futurist canvases at the Salon des Indépendents in Paris. Designs several propaganda posters in the style of the *lubok* (with texts by Mayakovsky) to support the Russian war effort against Germany and Austria.

1915 March-April: exhibits an important number of neo-primitive and alogist works (*The Aviator, An Englishman in Moscow*) at the Tramway V exhibition organized by Ivan Puni. Exter, Ivan Kliun, Morgunov, Nadezhda Udaltsova, Liubov Popova, Olga Rozanova and Tatlin also exhibit. Works on a new entirely abstract style during the summer which he decides to call Suprematism; a number of his Tramway V companions are instantly converted. Malevich, Puni, Kliun, Xenia Bogoslavskaya and Mikhail Menkova declare themselves to be Suprematists and publish their manifesto at the 0.10 Last Futurist Exhibition. Malevich's *Black Square* leaves critics and the public dumbfounded. Simultaneously publishes *From Cubism to Suprematism: New Painterly Realism,* a pamphlet which is reedited the following year. Larionov and Goncharova leave Russia permanently in June.

1916 Malevich exhibits only cubo-futurist and alogist works at the Store exhibition, Tatlin having refused to accept any suprematist works. Military duty at Smolensk. Collapse of project for the magazine *Supremus* with Malevich as director, Rozanova as chief editor, and Exter, Kliun, Matiushin and Popova as regular contributors. The suprematist group exhibits at the Knave of Diamonds exhibition this and the following year. A revised edition of *Du cubisme et du futurisme au suprématisme* is published in Moscow.

1917 Malevich registers with the Federation of Leftist Artists after the February uprisings. Appointed to oversee the national collections in the Kremlin after the October Revolution.

1918 Publishes a number of articles against the ultra-conservative cultural forces opposed to the Revolution in the March and April issues of *Anarkhia.* After the disappearance of this magazine, he contributes to *Iskusstvo kommuny.* Executes murals with Matiushin for the Congress of the Committee on Rural Poverty. With Pavel Mansurov's assistance designs the costumes for Mayakovsky's *Mystery Bouff,* directed by Meyerhold in Petrograd. Deeply affected by the death of Olga Rozanova.

1919 April: shows his *White on White* at the Tenth State Exhibition, Moscow. The suprematist group meets the opposition of Tatlin and the rising constructivist movement. Malevich moves away from Kliun and befriends Pevsner. Invited by El Lissitzky and Vera Ermolaeva to work at the Vitebsk School of Art, where Chagall is director. Leaves for Vitebsk, accompanied by his student and disciple Ilia Chashnik. Publishes his essay *On New Systems in Art,* which is reedited the following year in Moscow under the title of *From Cézanne to Suprematism.* Malevich exercises an extraordinary influence as both artist and professor.

Malevich solo exhibition, Moscow, 1919.

GINKhUK, c. 1925. Front row: N. Punin, V. Ermolaeva,
X. Ender, M. Matiushin, M. Ender and Malevich.
Standing behind Malevich: I. Chashnik and N. Suetin.

Kasimir Malevich, c. 1925.

1920 Founds Unovis at the Vitebsk School of Art with Lissitzky, Chashnik, Nina Kogan and Lazar Khidekel, much against the will of Chagall, who resigns. He wants to extend Suprematism to collective creations and changes the school syllabus with this in mind. His book *Suprematism: 34 Drawings* is published by Unovis. New performance of *Victory over the Sun* at Vitebsk with Ermolaeva's set design. A second Unovis opens at Smolensk.

1921 Malevich, who has abandoned painting, devotes himself to teaching, to theory and to the execution of his *Planits*. His teaching methods are contested within the school and by the municipal authorities. The Moscow INKhUK, influenced by the Constructivists, refuses its support. *A propos du problème de l'art plastique* is published in Smolensk.

1922 Publication of *God is not Cast Down. Art. The Church. The Factory* (Vitebsk). Leaves Vitebsk with a group of followers as optimum working conditions can no longer be provided. The Unovis members are welcomed at the Petrograd Museum for Artistic Culture. Malevich is reunited with his friend Matiushin, who is conducting visual research with Boris, Maria and Xenia Ender. Participates in the exhibition of Russian Art in Berlin during the autumn and in Amsterdam the following spring.

1923 The Unovis group shows a didactic collection of works at the exhibition of the Petrograd Artists of All Directions. Collaborates with the Lomonosov Porcelain Factory. Despite opposition to Suprematism in the press, Malevich is appointed head of four departments at the Museum of Artistic Culture. Death of his second wife. Begins to work on plaster *Architektons*.

1924 Petrograd Institute of Painterly Culture (GINKhUK) founded and directed by Malevich. Mansurov, Matiushin, Tatlin and Pavel Filonov are appointed heads of various departments. Several *Planits*, *Black Square*, *Black Circle* and *Black Cross* are shown at the XIV Venice Biennial.

1925 Work on the *Architektons* with Chashnik and Suetin. Marries Natalia Andreevna Manchenko. Tatlin abandons the INKhUK for the Moscow VKhutemas (Higher State Art Technical Studios).

1926 Dismissed as director of the GINKhUK, which is subsequently dissolved. The press violently attacks the work of the GINKhUK with the support of the conservative artists of the AKhRR.

1927 Lunacharsky, Commissar for public instruction, entrusts Malevich with the mission of representing the Leningrad Institute of Artistic Culture in Germany. Malevich hopes to be able to travel to Paris. He sets about producing a series of teaching charts to be used as visual aids for his lectures. Leaves Russia with an important stock of material. Spends March in Poland, where he is given an enthusiastic welcome thanks to the publicity Strzeminski, Kobro and Peiper have given him. Exhibition at the Polonia Hotel, Warsaw, and several banquets in his honour. Travels to the Dessau Bauhaus, directed by Walter Gropius, where he is given a warm welcome on 7th April and where Moholy-Nagy publishes a collection of his theoretical writings under the title of *Die gegendstanlose Welt*. He is given considerable space for a solo exhibition at the Grosse Berliner Kunstaustellung (7th May to 30th September). This is the main reason why he will leave behind, in the hands of Hugo Häring, a large number of paintings, *Architektons* and documents which he had brought with him. In Berlin, meets Arp, Schwitters (with whom he disagrees) and Hans Richter, who proposes that they make a film (only Malevich's scenario would be written). Returns to Leningrad on 6th June to resume his research at the State Institute for the History of Art, and to continue working on the *Architektons* with Suetin and Chashnik.

1928 Confrontation with the Constructivists. Important article, "Form, Colour and Sensation," published in the Moscow review *Contemporary Architecture;* it would be Malevich's last publication in Russian. Begins a three-year collaboration with the Ukrainian magazine *Nova Generatsiya,* where he explains recent artistic development since Cézanne.

Reception in honour of Malevich, Warsaw, 1927.

Malevich lying in state.

Malevich's solo exhibition, Berlin, 1927. Note different orientation of *Supremus no. 50.*

1929 Malevich and his department are expelled by the authorities of the State Institute for the History of Art, Leningrad. Works for two and a half weeks per month at the Art Institute, Kiev. The State Tretyakov Gallery, Moscow, organizes a retrospective of his work in November. Malevich repaints a number of past works which he needs for the exhibition and antedates them. His disciple Ilya Chashnik dies.

1930 The Kiev Municipal Museum shows a modified version of the 1929 Moscow exhibition. Malevich teaches a course on the Theory of Painting at the Leningrad House of Art. He is arrested and held for several days for questioning. As a precautionary measure, his friends destroy a number of his papers.

1931 Executes a painting for the interior of the Red Theatre, Leningrad.

1932 The Russian Museum, Leningrad, appoints him to a Research Laboratory post, which he occupies until his death. A state decree obliges all artistic groups to merge within a single Union where avant-garde tendencies are stifled. Extensive show of Malevich's work (*Architektons* and paintings including the recent faceless figures) at the Artists of the RSFSR over a Period of Fifteen Years exhibition at Leningrad and Moscow.

1933 Malevich writes an important autobiography. Paints his own *Self-Portrait* and several portraits of his family and close friends in a renaissance style.

1934 Surrounded by the affection of his disciples, but terminally ill, Malevich is hardly able to paint. His old friend Matiushin dies.

1935 Five recent portraits are presented at the First Exhibition of Leningrad Artists; this was the last public show in the Soviet Union of any of Malevich's work until 1962. Dies 15th May. The town of Leningrad arranges for his funeral; a large part of his studio and estate is placed under the care of the State Russian Museum and a state pension is awarded to his family. After lying in state surrounded by works from different periods, the painter's remains are placed in a suprematist-style coffin designed by Suetin. A huge funeral procession accompanies the lorry, adorned with *Black Square,* which bears the coffin. Malevich's remains are transported by train to Moscow and then to Nemchinovska, where his ashes are finally buried in a field next to his *dacha.* Suetin adorns the tomb with a cube and a black square.

SELECTED BIBLIOGRAPHY

WRITINGS BY MALEVICH

Collected works in English translation edited by Troels Andersen:
Essays on Art, 1915-1933, 2 vols., ed. Troels Andersen, trans. Xenia Glowacki-Prus and Arnold McMillin, London, Rapp and Whiting, 1968.
The World as Non-Objectivity: Unpublished Writings, 1922-1925, ed. Troels Andersen, trans. Xenia Glowacki-Prus and Edmund T. Little, Copenhagen, Borlen, 1976.
The Artist, Infinity, Suprematism: Unpublished Writings, 1913-1933, ed. Troels Andersen, trans. Xebnia Hoffmann, Copenhagen, Borlen, 1978.

Collected works in French translation edited by Jean-Claude Marcadé:
Écrits I : De Cézanne au suprématisme: Tous les traités parus de 1915 à 1922, ed. and trans. by J.C. and V. Marcadé, Lausanne, L'Age d'Homme, 1974.
Écrits II : Le Miroir suprématiste: Tous les articles parus en russe de 1913 à 1928, avec des documents sur le suprématisme, ed. and trans. by J.C. and V. Marcadé, Lausanne, L'Age d'Homme, 1977.
Écrits III : Izoologia, Les Arts de la représentation, (forthcoming).
Écrits IV : La Lumière et la Couleur: textes inédites de 1918 à 1926 ed. and trans. by J.C. and V. Marcadé, Lausanne, L'Age d'Homme, 1981.

Selected works:
Écrits, ed. by Andréi B. Nakov, Paris, Champ Libre, 1975.

PRINCIPAL BOOKS AND CATALOGUES

Gray, Camilla, *The Great Experiment: Russian Art, 1863-1922,* London, Thames & Hudson, 1962. (Revised and enlarged edition, *The Russian Experiment in Art, 1863-1922,* London, Thames & Hudson, 1986.)

Markov, Vladimir, *Russian Futurism,* Berkeley, University of California Press, 1968.

Andersen, Troels, *Malévitch : Catalogue Raisonné of the Berlin Exhibition of 1927,* Amsterdam, Stedelijk Museum, 1970.

Marcadé, Valentine, *Le Renouveau de l'art pictural russe, 1863-1914,* Lausanne, L'Age d'Homme, 1971.

Manifestes futuristes russes, Robel, Léon, ed. and trans., Paris, Les Editeurs Français Réunis, 1971.

Russian Art of the Avant-Garde, Bowlt, John E., ed. New York, Viking Press, 1976.

Kroutchenykh, A., Matiouchine, M., *La Victoire sur le soleil,* trans. J.-C. and V. Marcadé, Lausanne, L'Age d'Homme, 1976.

Martineau, Emmanuel, *Malévitch et la philosophie,* Lausanne, L'Age d'Homme, 1977.

Malévitch, exhibition catalogue, Paris, Centre Georges-Pompidou, 1978.

Compton, Susan P., *The World Backwards : Russian Futurist Books 1912-1916,* London, The British Library, 1978.

Shadowa, Larissa A., *Suche und Experiment : Russische und Sovietische Kunst 1910 bis 1930,* Dresden, Verlag der Kunst, 1978. (English translation: Zhadova, L. *Malevich: Suprematism and Revolution in Russian Art, 1910-1930,* trans. A. Lieven, London, Thames & Hudson, 1982.)

Marcadé, J.C., ed., *Malévitch, 1878-1935: Actes du colloque international tenu au Centre Pompidou, Musée National d'Art Moderne, les 4 et 5 mai 1978,* Lausanne, L'Age d'Homme, 1979.

Fauchereau, Serge, *L'Avant-garde russe,* Paris, Belfond, 1979.

Paris-Moscou 1900-1930, exhibition catalogue, Paris, Centre Georges-Pompidou, 1979.

Malévitch : Architectones, Peintures, Dessins, Paris, Centre Georges-Pompidou, 1980.

Zander-Rudenstine, Angelica, *Russian Avant-Garde : The George Costakis Collection,* New York, Abrams, 1981.

Nakov, Andréi B., *Abstrait/Concret: art non-objectif russe et polonais,* Paris, Transédition, 1981.

Cardoza y Aragón, Luis, *Malévitch,* Universidad Nacional Autónoma de México, 1983.

Fauchereau, Serge, ed., *Moscou 1900-1930,* Paris, Seuil, 1988.

Kazimir Malévitch, exhibition catalogue, Leningrad, State Russian Museum/Moscow, Tretyakov Gallery/Amsterdam, Stedelijk Museum, 1988-89.

Art and Design "Malevich," vol. 5, no. 5-6, London, 1989.

Railing, Patricia, *On Suprematism : 34 Drawings,* Forest Row, G. B., 1990.

Petrova, Evgénia, *Malévitch,* Paris, Flammarion, 1990.

Marcadé, Jean-Claude, *Malévitch,* Paris, Nouvelles Editions Françaises-Casterman, 1990.

Kazimir Malévitch 1878-1935, exhibition catalogue, Washington, D.C., National Gallery of Art / Los Angeles, Armand Hammer Museum and Cultural Centre / New York, The Metropolitan Museum of Art, 1990.

PLATES

1. *Portrait of a Member of the Artist's Family,* 1906.
   Oil on canvas mounted on wood, 26¾×39 in. (68×99 cm).
   Stedelijk Museum, Amsterdam.

2. *Landscape,* 1906–7.
   Oil on canvas mounted on wood, 7½×12¼ in. (19.2×31 cm).
   State Russian Museum, Leningrad.

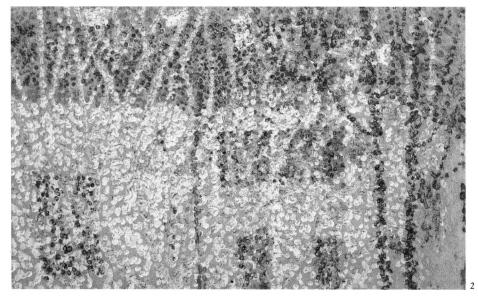

1

2

3. *Study for a Fresco (Self-Portrait),* 1907.
   Tempera on cardboard, 27¼×27⅜ in. (69.3×70 cm).
   State Russian Museum, Leningrad.

3

4. *Study for a Fresco,* 1907.
   Tempera on cardboard, 28½×27⅜ in. (72.5×70 cm).
   State Russian Museum, Leningrad.

4

5. *Study for a Fresco*, 1907.
   Tempera on cardboard, 27⅝×29½ in. (70×74.8 cm).
   State Russian Museum, Leningrad.

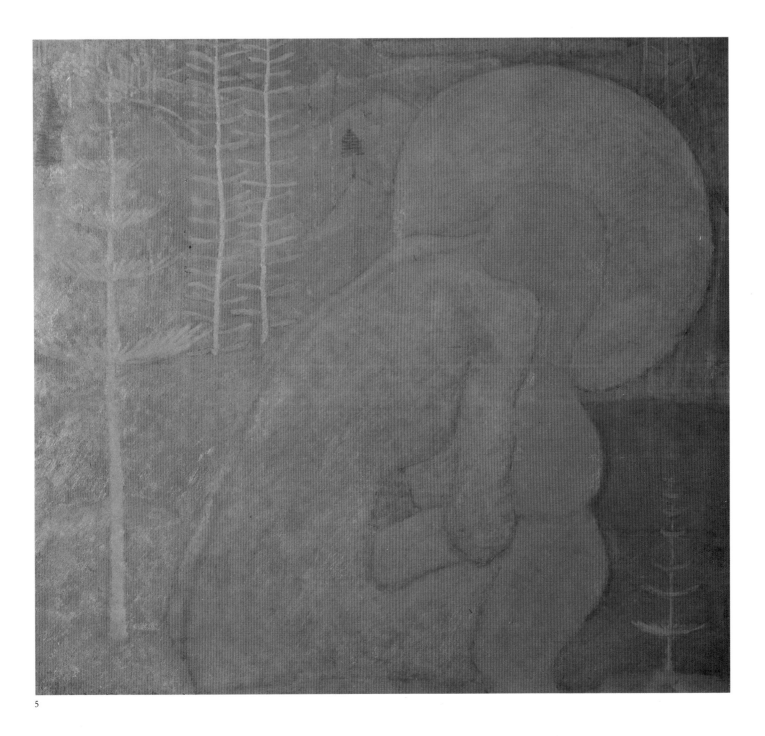

5

6. *Study for a Fresco,* 1907.
   Tempera on cardboard, 27¼×28⅛ in. (69.3×71.5 cm).
   State Russian Museum, Leningrad.

6

7. *Relaxing: High Society in Top Hats,* 1908.
   Gouache, watercolour and India ink on cardboard, 9⅜×12 in. (23.8×30.2 cm).
   State Russian Museum, Leningrad.

7

8. *Bathing Women*, 1908?
   Oil on canvas, 23¼×18⅞ in. (59×48 cm).
   State Russian Museum, Leningrad.

9. *Landscape with Red Houses,* 1910–11.
   Gouache, 42⅛×41¾ in. (107×106 cm).
   Kunstmuseum, Basel.

9

10. *Bather*, 1911.
    Gouache on paper, 41⅜×27⅛ in. (105×69 cm).
    Stedelijk Museum, Amsterdam.

11. *The Gardener*, 1911.
    Charcoal and gouache on paper, 35⅞×27⅝ in. (91×70 cm).
    Stedelijk Museum, Amsterdam.

12

13

12. *On the Boulevard,* 1911.
    Charcoal and gouache on paper, 28⅜×28 in. (72×71 cm).
    Stedelijk Museum, Amsterdam.

13. *Woman with Buckets and Child,* 1912.
    Oil on canvas, 28¾×28¾ in. (73×73 cm).
    Stedelijk Museum, Amsterdam.

14. *Peasant Woman with Buckets: Dynamic arrangement,* 1912–13.
    Oil on canvas, 31⅝×31⅝ in. (80.3×80.3 cm).
    The Museum of Modern Art, New York.

15. *Taking in the Rye,* 1912.
    Oil on canvas, 28⅜×29⅜ in. (72×74.5 cm).
    Stedelijk Museum, Amsterdam.

15

16. *Reaping Woman*, 1912.
Oil on canvas, 28¾×27⅝ in. (73×70 cm).
Astrakhan Museum.

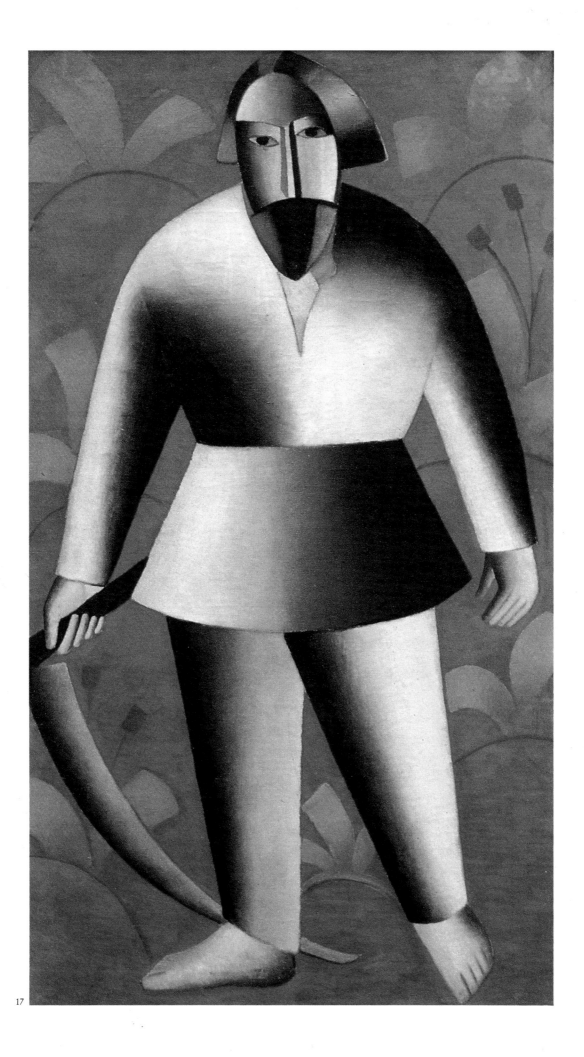

17

17. *Reaper on Red Background,* 1912–13.
    Oil on canvas, 45¼×27⅛ in. (115×69 cm).
    Fine Arts Museum, Gorki.

18. *The Knife Grinder,* 1912–13.
    Oil on canvas, 31¼×31¼ in. (79.5×79.5 cm).
    Yale University Art Gallery, New Haven.

18

19. *Head of a Peasant Girl,* 1912–13.
    Oil on canvas, 31½×37⅜ in. (80×95 cm).
    Stedelijk Museum, Amsterdam.

20. *Portrait of Ivan Kliun,* 1913.
    Oil on canvas, 44⅛×27⅝ in. (112×70 cm).
    State Russian Museum, Leningrad.

19

21. *Through Station: Kuntsevo*, 1913.
Oil on wooden panel,
19¼×10 in. (49×25.5 cm).
State Tretyakov Gallery, Moscow.

21

22

23. *Death of a Man Simultaneously in an Aeroplane and on a Railway,* lithograph for Alexis Kruchenykh's book *Explodity,* 1913. 3⅝×5½ in. (9.1×14 cm).

24. *Three,* 1913.
Cover, lithograph,
7½×6½ in. (18.5×16.5 cm).
Private collection.

25. Illustration from *A Game in Hell,* by V. Khlebnikov and A. Kruchenykh.

23

24

25

26. *Portrait of M. V. Matiushin*, 1913.
    Oil on canvas, 41⅞×41⅞ in. (106.3×106.3 cm).
    State Tretyakov Gallery, Moscow.

26

27. *Soldier of the First Division*, 1914.
    Oil and collage on canvas, 21⅛×17⅝ in. (53.6×44.8 cm).
    The Museum of Modern Art, New York.

28. *Composition with Mona Lisa,* 1914.
    Oil and collage on canvas, 24¾×19½ in. (62×49.5 cm).
    State Russian Museum, Leningrad.

29. *An Englishman in Moscow,* 1914.
    Oil on canvas, 34⅝×22½ in. (88×57 cm).
    Stedelijk Museum, Amsterdam.

30. *The Aviator,* 1914.
    Oil on canvas, 49¼×25⅝ in. (125×65 cm).
    State Tretyakov Gallery, Moscow.

28. *Composition with Mona Lisa,* 1914.
Oil and collage on canvas, 24¼×19½ in. (62×49.5 cm).
State Russian Museum, Leningrad.

29. *An Englishman in Moscow,* 1914.
    Oil on canvas, 34⅝×22½ in. (88×57 cm).
    Stedelijk Museum, Amsterdam.

30. *The Aviator,* 1914.
    Oil on canvas, 49¼×25⅝ in. (125×65 cm).
    State Tretyakov Gallery, Moscow.

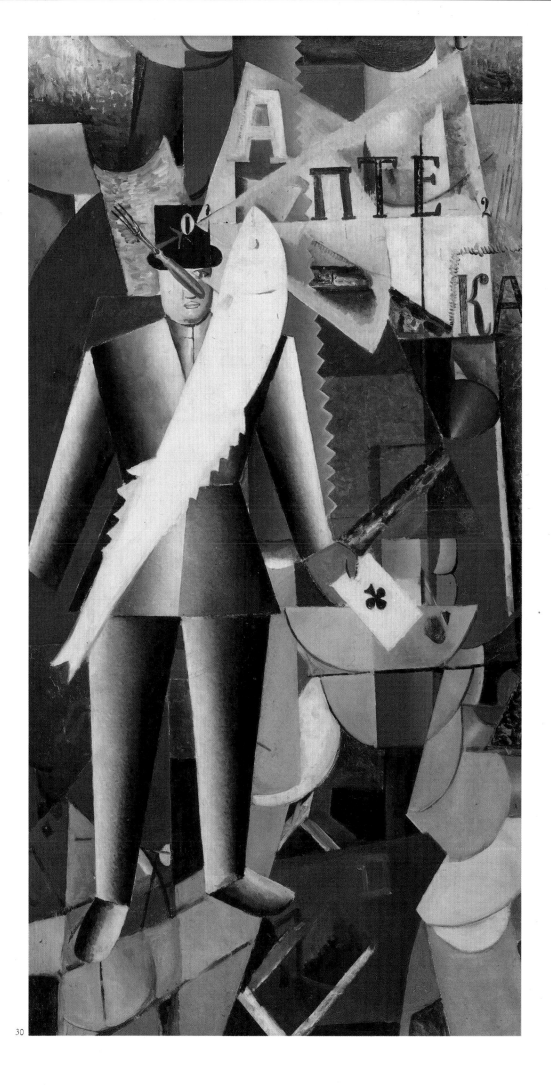

31. *Black Square* [1913] 1923–29.
    Oil on canvas, 41¾×41⅞ in. (106.2×106.5 cm).
    State Russian Museum, Leningrad.

31

32. *Black Circle* [1913] 1923–29.
Oil on canvas, 41½×41½ in. (105.5×105.5 cm).
State Russian Museum, Leningrad.

33. *Black Cross* [1913] 1923–29.
   Oil on canvas, 41⅞×41⅞ in. (106.4×106.4 cm).
   State Russian Museum, Leningrad.

34. *Red Square: Painterly Realism of a Peasant Woman in Two Dimensions,* 1915.
Oil on canvas, 20⅞×20⅞ in. (53×53 cm).
State Russian Museum, Leningrad.

35. *Suprematism: Self-Portrait in Two Dimensions*, 1915.
Oil on canvas, 31½×24⅜ in. (80×62 cm).
Stedelijk Museum, Amsterdam.

36. *Suprematist Painting: Aeroplane Flying*, 1915.
Oil on canvas, 22⅜×19 in. (57.3×48.3 cm).
The Museum of Modern Art, New York.

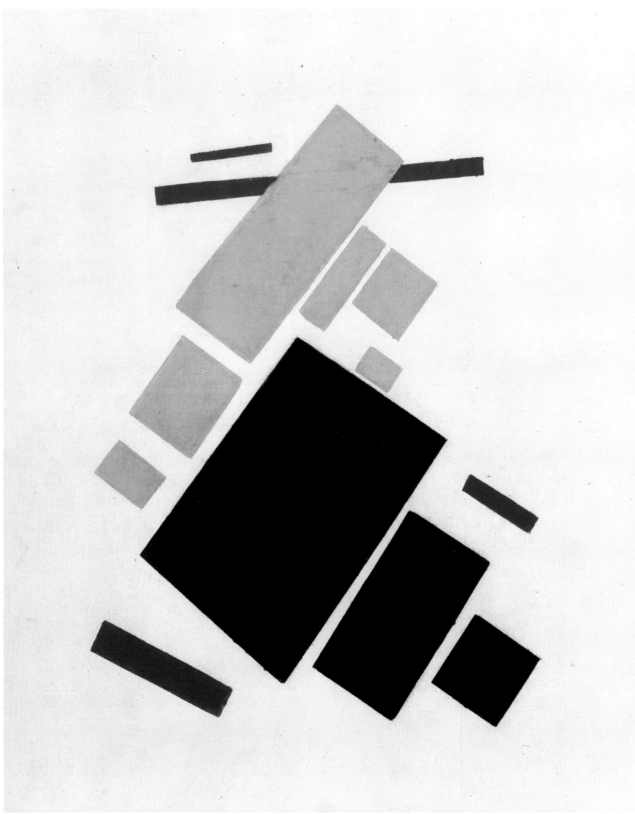

37. *Suprematism,* 1915.
    Oil on canvas, 34½×28⅜ in. (87.5×72 cm).
    State Russian Museum, Leningrad.

38. *Black Square and Red Square,* 1915.
    Oil on canvas, 28×17½ in. (71.1×44.4 cm).
    The Museum of Modern Art, New York.

39. *Suprematist Composition,* 1915.
   Oil on canvas, 27⅝×18½ in. (70×47 cm).
   Fine Arts Museum, Tula.

39

40. *Suprematism*, 1916–17.
   Oil on canvas, 31½×31½ in. (80×80 cm).
   Fine Arts Museum, Krasnodar.

41. *Supremus No. 56*, 1916.
    Oil on canvas, 31¼×28 in. (80.5×71 cm).
    State Russian Museum, Leningrad.

42. *Suprematism (Supremus No. 58),* 1916.
Oil on canvas, 31¼×27¾ in. (79.5×70.5 cm).
State Russian Museum, Leningrad.

43. *Suprematist Painting*, 1916.
    Oil on canvas, 34⅝×27⅝ in. (88×70 cm).
    Stedelijk Museum, Amsterdam.

43

44. *Suprematist Painting*, 1915–16.
Oil on canvas, 19¼×17⅜ in. (49×44 cm).
Wilhelm Hacke Museum, Ludwigshafen.

45

45. *Suprematist Painting,* 1917.
    Oil on canvas, 38×25¾ in. (96.5×65.4 cm).
    The Museum of Modern Art, New York.

46. *Suprematist Painting: Yellow Quadrilateral on White,* 1917–18.
    Oil on canvas, 41¾×27¾ in. (106×70.5 cm).
    Stedelijk Museum, Amsterdam.

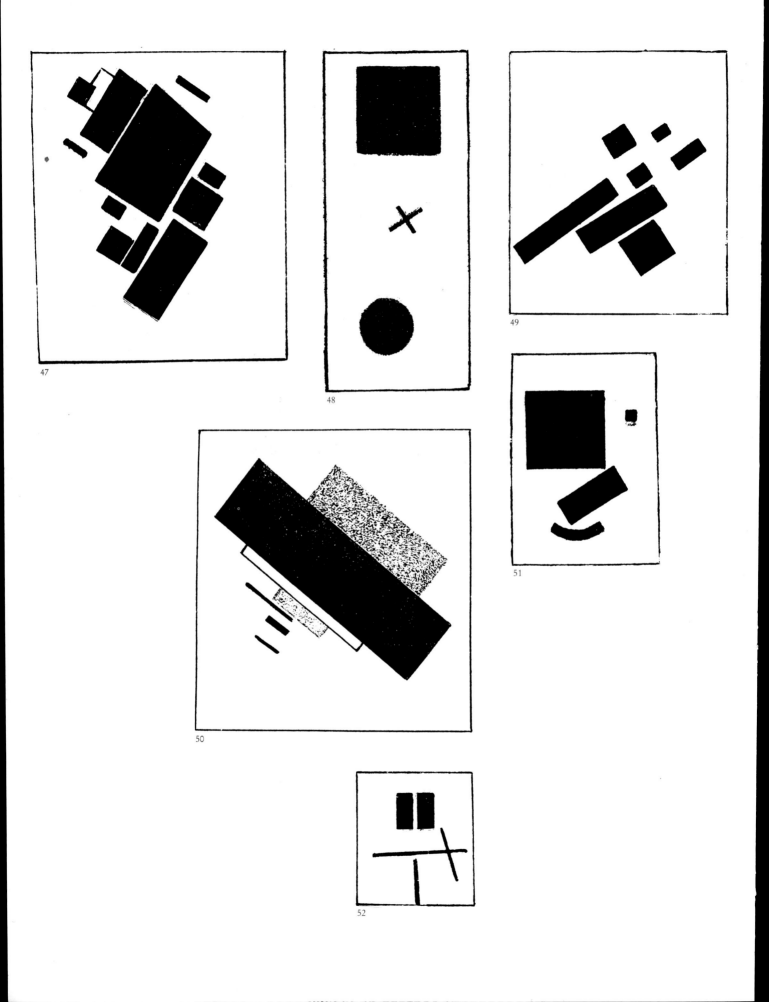

47

48

49

50

51

52

53

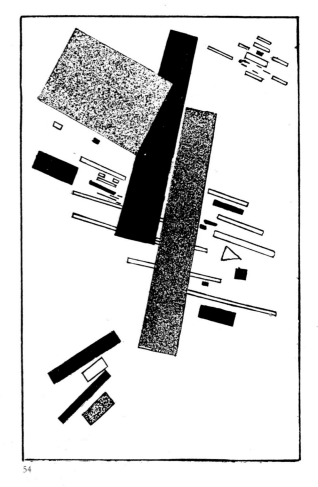

54

55. *Suprematism: White on White,* 1918.
Oil on canvas,
31×31 in. (78.7×78.7 cm).
The Museum of Modern Art, New York.

56. *Suprematist Painting,* 1920–25.
Oil on canvas,
31¼×31¼ in. (79.3×79.3 cm).
The Museum of Modern Art, New York.

55

56

57. *Future Planits for Leningrad. The Pilot's House*, 1924.
    Pencil on paper, 12×17¾ in. (30.5×45 cm).
    Stedelijk Museum, Amsterdam.

58. *Future Planits for Earth Dwellers*, 1923–24.
    Pencil on paper, 17⅜×12⅛ in. (44×30.8 cm).
    Stedelijk Museum, Amsterdam.

59. *Modern Buildings*, 1922–24.
    Pencil on paper, 14⅛×21⅛ in. (36×53.5 cm).
    Stedelijk Museum, Amsterdam.

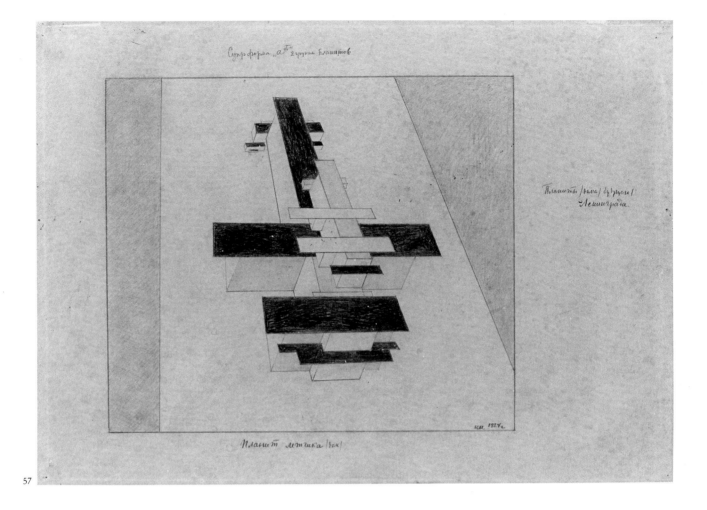

57

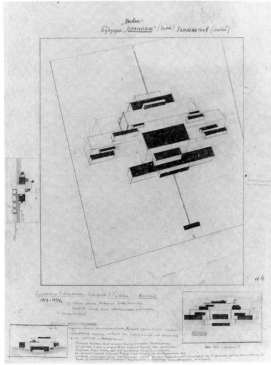

58

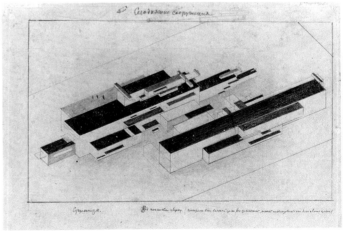

59

60. *Gota*, 1923?
    Plaster, 33½×18⅞×22⅞ in. (85.2×48×58 cm).
    Musée National d'Art Moderne, Paris.

61. *Zeta*, 1923–27.
    Plaster, 31¼×22⅜×28⅛ in. (79.4×56.7×71.4 cm).
    Musée National d'Art Moderne, Paris.

62. *Suprematist Ornaments*, 1927.
    18 plaster elements, overall dimension at base,
    17¾×23⅝ in. (45×60 cm).
    Musée National d'Art Moderne, Paris.

60

61

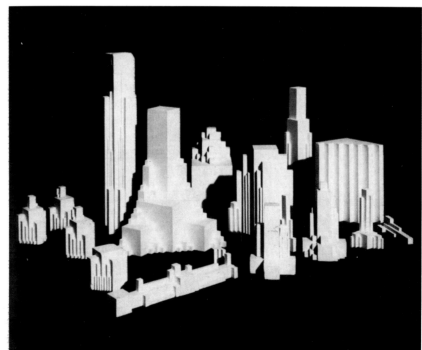

62

63. *Beta*, before 1926.
   Plaster, 10¾×23⅜×39⅛ in. (27.3×59.5×99.3 cm).
   Musée National d'Art Moderne, Paris.

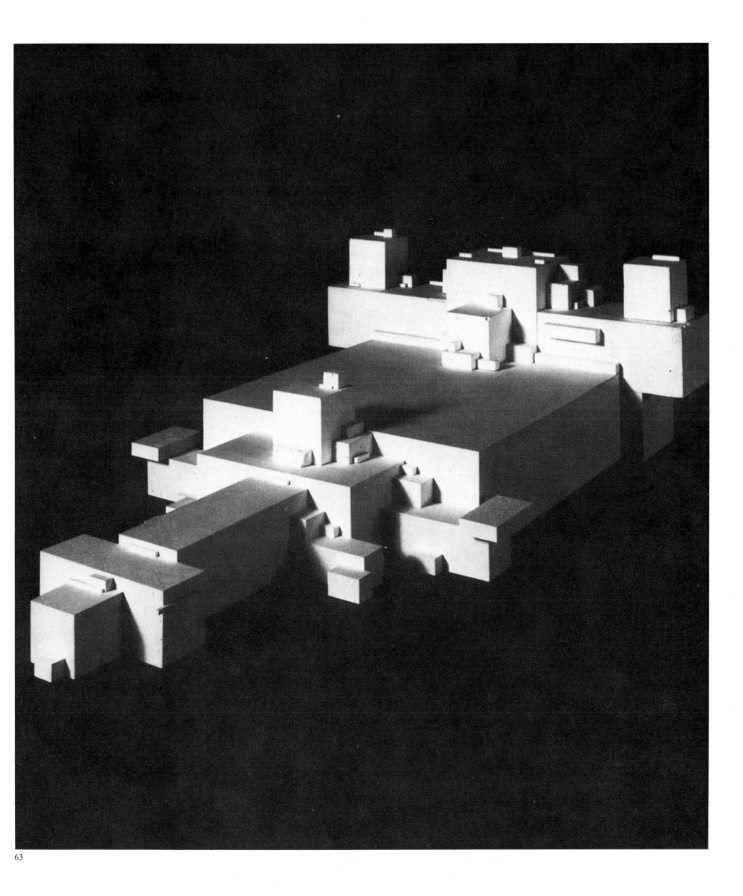

64. *Jobless Girl* [1904].
Oil on canvas, 31½×26 in. (80×66 cm).
State Russian Museum, Leningrad.

65. *Spring,* after 1927.
    Oil on canvas, 20⅞×26 in. (53×66 cm).
    State Russian Museum, Leningrad.

66. *Reapers,* after 1927.
    Oil on wood, 28×40⅝ in. (71×103.2 cm).
    State Russian Museum, Leningrad.

65

66

67. *Woman with a Yellow Hat* [1908].
Oil on canvas, 18⅞×15⅜ in. (48×39 cm).
State Russian Museum, Leningrad.

68. *Carpenter*, 1927.
   Oil on plyboard, 28⅜×21¼ in. (72×54 cm).
   State Russian Museum, Leningrad.

69

70

69. *At the Dacha*, after 1928.
   Oil on wood, 42½×28⅜ in. (108×72 cm).
   State Russian Museum, Leningrad.

70. *The Harvest*, after 1928.
   Oil on wood, 28⅜×20¾ in. (72.8×52.8 cm).
   State Russian Museum, Leningrad.

71. *Small Boy (Vanka)*, after 1927.
   Oil on canvas, 28⅜×20¼ in. (72×51.5 cm).
   State Russian Museum, Leningrad.

72

73

72. *At the Harvest (Marfa and Vanka),* after 1927.
  Oil on canvas, 32¼×24 in. (82×61 cm).
  State Russian Museum, Leningrad.

73. *Reaper,* 1928-30.
  Oil on canvas, 33¾×25⅞ in. (85.8×65.6 cm).
  State Russian Museum, Leningrad.

74. *Head of a Peasant,* 1928-30?
  Oil on plywood, 28¼×21⅛ in. (71.7×53.8 cm).
  State Russian Museum, Leningrad.

75. *Peasant in the Fields,* 1928–30?
    Oil on plywood, 28⅛×17⅜ in. (71.3×44.2 cm).
    State Russian Museum, Leningrad.

76. *Girls in the Field,* 1928–30.
    Oil on canvas, 41¾×49¼ in. (106×125 cm).
    State Russian Museum, Leningrad.

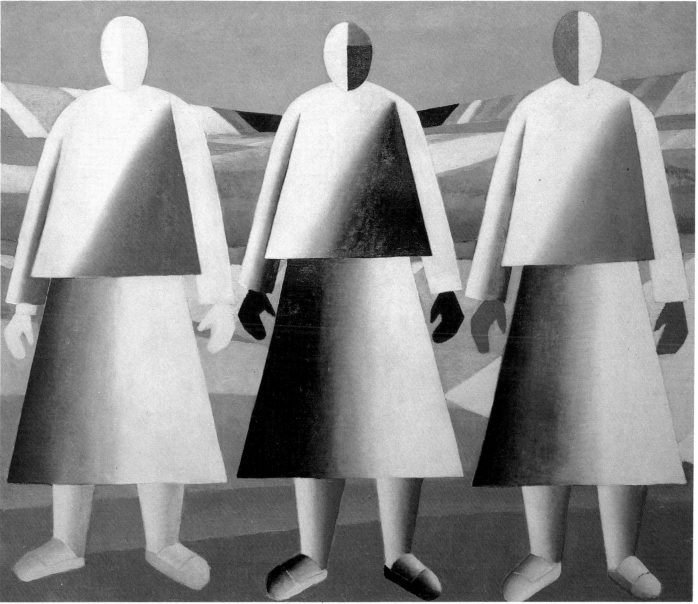

76

77. *Complex Presentiment: Half-Figure in a Yellow Shirt*, 1928-32.
Oil on canvas, 39×31⅛ in. (99×79 cm).
State Russian Museum, Leningrad.

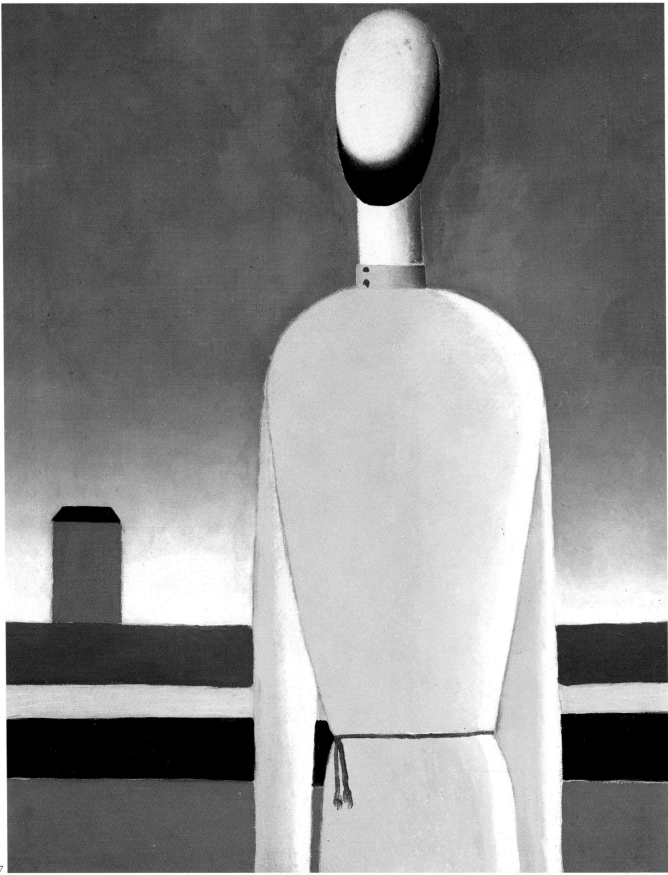

78. *Peasant Woman*, 1929–30?
    Oil on canvas, 38¾×31½ in. (98.5×80 cm).
    State Russian Museum, Leningrad.

79. *Two Peasants,* 1928–32.
Oil on canvas, 20⅞×27⅝ in. (53×70 cm).
State Russian Museum, Leningrad.

80. *Three Female Figures,* 1928–30.
Oil on canvas, 18½×25 in. (47×63.5 cm).
State Russian Museum, Leningrad.

79

80

81. *Sportsmen*, 1928–30.
Oil on canvas, 55⅞×64⅝ in. (142×164 cm).
State Russian Museum, Leningrad.

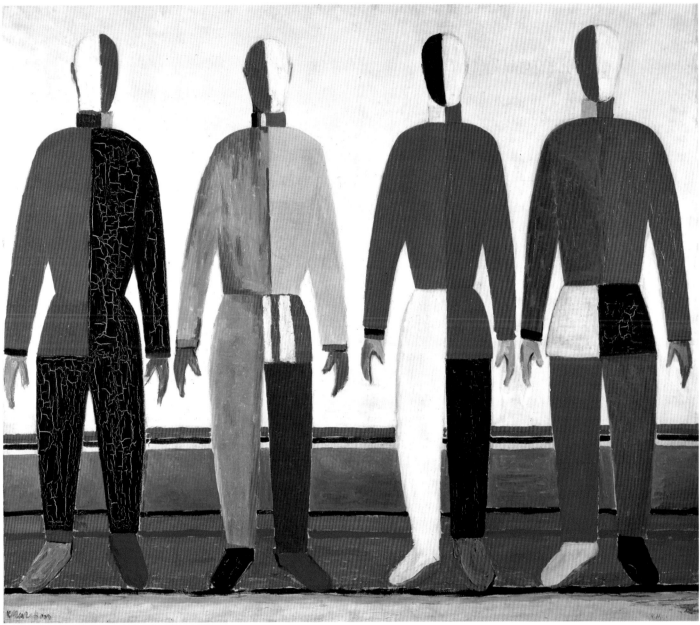

81

82. *Red Cavalry,* 1930–31.
    Oil on canvas, 35⅞×55⅛ in. (91×140 cm).
    State Russian Museum, Leningrad.

83. *Landscape with a White House, c.* 1930.
    Oil on canvas, 23¼×23½ in. (59×59.6 cm).
    State Russian Museum, Leningrad.

84. *Landscape with Five Houses, c.* 1932.
    Oil on canvas, 32⅝×24⅜ in. (83×62 cm).
    State Russian Museum, Leningrad.

82

83

84

85. *Red House,* 1932.
Oil on canvas, 24¼×21⅝ in. (63×55 cm).
State Russian Museum, Leningrad.

86. *Torso: Half-Figure with a Pink Face*, 1928–32.
    Oil on canvas, 28⅜×25⅝ in. (72×65 cm).
    State Russian Museum, Leningrad.

87. *Half-Figure (Prototype of a New Image)*, 1928–32.
    Oil on canvas, 18⅛×14⅝ in. (46×37 cm).
    State Russian Museum, Leningrad.

88. *Female Portrait,* 1928–32.
   Oil on plywood, 22⅞×19¼ in. (58×49 cm).
   State Russian Museum, Leningrad.

89. *Three Women,* 1928–32.
   Oil on wood, 22½×18⅞ in. (57×48 cm).
   State Russian Museum, Leningrad.

90. *Female Half-Figure,* 1928–32.
   Oil on wood.
   State Russian Museum, Leningrad.

88

89

90

91. *Two Male Figures,* 1930–32.
Oil on canvas, 39×29⅛ in. (99×74 cm).
State Russian Museum, Leningrad.

92. *Peasant,* 1928–32.
Oil on canvas, 47¼×39⅜ in. (120×100 cm).
State Russian Museum, Leningrad.

93. *Bathers,* 1928–32.
Oil on canvas, 38¾×31⅛ in. (98.5×79 cm).
State Russian Museum, Leningrad.

92

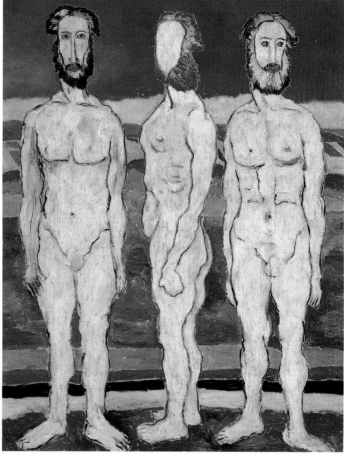

93

94. *Five Figures with Hammer and Sickle, c.* 1930–32.
Pen and ink on paper, 3×4¼ in. (7.6×12 cm).
Musée National d'Art Moderne, Paris.

96. *Running Man,* 1932–34.
Oil on canvas, 31⅛×25⅝ in. (79×65 cm).
Musée National d'Art Moderne, Paris.

95. *The Arrest. Man and Power,* after 1930.
Pencil on paper, 13×8½ in. (33×21.7 cm).
Private collection.

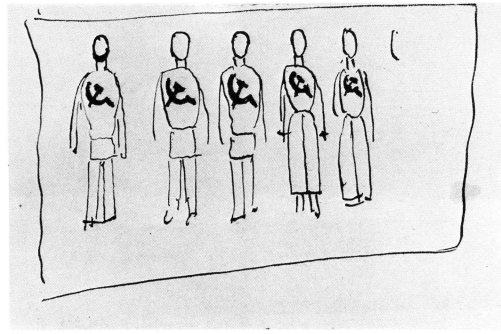

94

95

97. *Head of a Young Girl of Today,* 1932.
Oil on canvas, 17⅛×13⅜ in. (43.5×34 cm).
State Russian Museum, Leningrad.

98. *Girl with Comb in Hair,* 1932–33.
    Oil on canvas, 14×12¼ in. (35.5×31 cm).
    State Tretyakov Gallery, Moscow.

99. *Girl with Red Pole*, 1932–33.
    Oil on canvas, 28×24 in. (71×61 cm).
    State Tretyakov Gallery, Moscow.

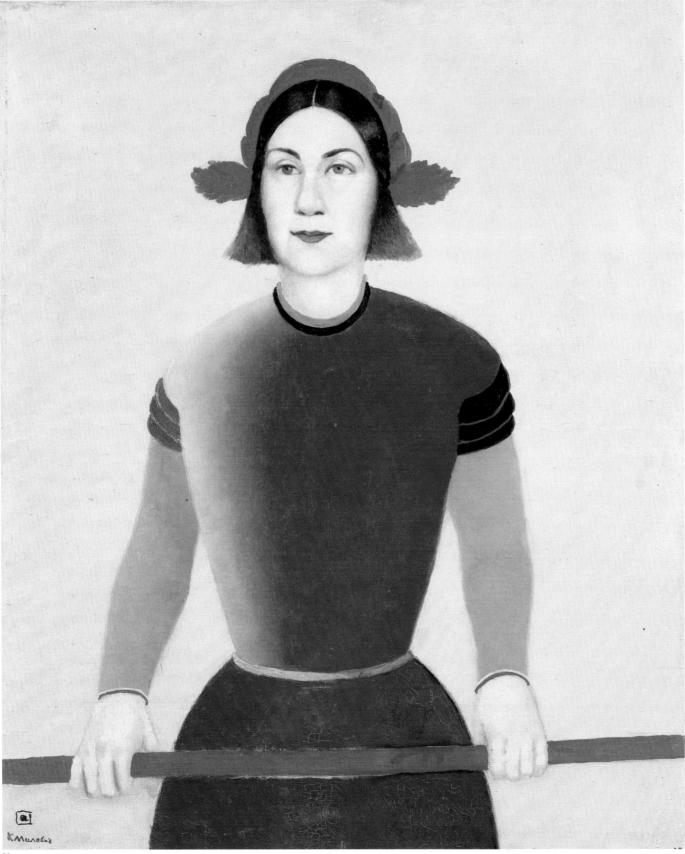

100. *Male Portrait (N. Punin?)*, 1933.
Oil on canvas, 28×22½ in. (71×57 cm).
State Russian Museum, Leningrad.

101. *Portrait of the Artist's Wife*, 1933.
Oil on canvas, 26⅜×22 in. (67.5×56 cm).
State Russian Museum, Leningrad.

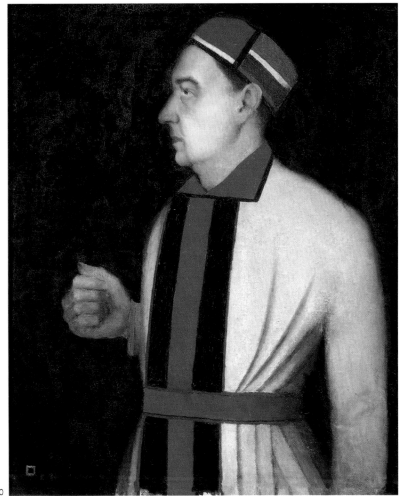

100

101

102. *Portrait of Una, c.* 1932.
Oil on canvas, 20½×16¾ in. (52×42.4 cm).
Moderna Museet, Stockholm.

103. *Female Worker*, 1933.
Oil on canvas, 28×23½ in. (71.2×59.8 cm).
State Russian Museum, Leningrad.

104. *Portrait of the Artist's Daughter*, 1933–34.
     Oil on canvas, 33½×24⅜ in. (85×61.8 cm).
     State Russian Museum, Leningrad.

105. *Portrait of the Artist's Wife*, 1934.
     Oil on canvas, 39⅛×29¼ in. (99.5×74.3 cm).
     State Russian Museum, Leningrad.

104

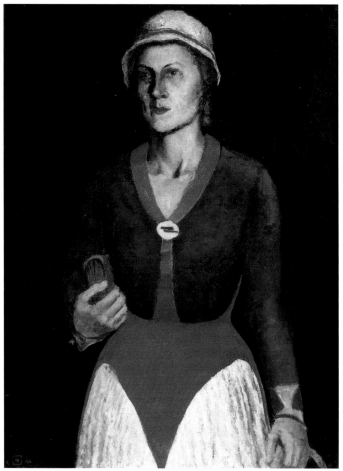

105

106. *Self-Portrait*, 1933.
Oil on canvas, 28¾×26 in. (73×66 cm).
State Russian Museum, Leningrad.

LIST OF PLATES

1. *Portrait of a Member of the Artist's Family,* 1906.
   Oil on canvas mounted on wood,
   26¾×39 in. (68×99 cm).
   Stedelijk Museum, Amsterdam.

2. *Landscape,* 1906–7.
   Oil on canvas mounted on wood,
   7½×12¼ in. (19.2×31 cm).
   State Russian Museum, Leningrad.

3. *Study for a Fresco (Self-Portrait),* 1907.
   Tempera on cardboard,
   27¼×27⅝ in. (69.3×70 cm).
   State Russian Museum, Leningrad.

4. *Study for a Fresco,* 1907.
   Tempera on cardboard,
   28½×27⅝ in. (72.5×70 cm).
   State Russian Museum, Leningrad.

5. *Study for a Fresco,* 1907.
   Tempera on cardboard,
   27⅝×29½ in. (70×74.8 cm).
   State Russian Museum, Leningrad.

6. *Study for a Fresco,* 1907.
   Tempera on cardboard,
   27¼×28⅛ in. (69.3×71.5 cm).
   State Russian Museum, Leningrad.

7. *Relaxing: High Society in Top Hats,* 1908.
   Gouache, watercolour and India ink on cardboard,
   9⅜×12 in. (23.8×30.2 cm).
   State Russian Museum, Leningrad.

8. *Bathing Women,* 1908?
   Oil on canvas,
   23¼×18⅞ in. (59×48 cm).
   State Russian Museum, Leningrad.

9. *Landscape with Red Houses,* 1910–11.
   Gouache,
   42⅛×41¾ in. (107×106 cm).
   Kunstmuseum, Basel.

10. *Bather,* 1911.
    Gouache on paper,
    41⅜×27⅛ in. (105×69 cm).
    Stedelijk Museum, Amsterdam.

11. *The Gardener,* 1911.
    Charcoal and gouache on paper,
    35⅞×27⅝ in. (91×70 cm).
    Stedelijk Museum, Amsterdam.

12. *On the Boulevard,* 1911.
    Charcoal and gouache on paper,
    28⅜×28 in. (72×71 cm).
    Stedelijk Museum, Amsterdam.

13. *Woman with Buckets and Child,* 1912.
    Oil on canvas,
    28¾×28¾ in. (73×73 cm).
    Stedelijk Museum, Amsterdam.

14. *Peasant Woman with Buckets: Dynamic arrangement,* 1912–13.
    Oil on canvas,
    31⅝×31⅝ in. (80.3×80.3 cm).
    The Museum of Modern Art, New York.

15. *Taking in the Rye,* 1912.
    Oil on canvas,
    28⅜×29⅜ in. (72×74.5 cm).
    Stedelijk Museum, Amsterdam.

16. *Reaping Woman,* 1912.
    Oil on canvas,
    28¾×27⅝ in. (73×70 cm).
    Astrakhan Museum.

17. *Reaper on Red Background,* 1912–13.
    Oil on canvas,
    45¼×27⅛ in. (115×69 cm).
    Fine Arts Museum, Gorki.

18. *The Knife Grinder,* 1912–13.
    Oil on canvas,
    31¼×31¼ in. (79.5×79.5 cm).
    Yale University Art Gallery, New Haven.

19. *Head of a Peasant Girl,* 1912–13.
    Oil on canvas,
    31½×37⅜ in. (80×95 cm).
    Stedelijk Museum, Amsterdam.

20. *Portrait of Ivan Kliun,* 1913.
    Oil on canvas,
    44⅛×27⅝ in. (112×70 cm).
    State Russian Museum, Leningrad.

21. *Through Station: Kuntsevo,* 1913.
    Oil on wooden panel,
    19¼×10 in. (49×25.5 cm).
    State Tretyakov Gallery, Moscow.

22. *Cow and Violin,* 1913.
    Oil on wooden panel,
    19¼×10⅛ in. (48.9×25.8 cm).
    State Russian Museum, Leningrad.

23. *Death of a Man Simultaneously in an Aeroplane and on a Railway,*
    lithograph for Alexis Kruchenykh's book *Explodity,* 1913.
    3⅝×5½ in. (9.1×14 cm).

24. *Three,* 1913.
    Cover, lithograph,
    7½×6½ in. (18.5×16.5 cm).
    Private collection.

25. Illustration from *A Game in Hell,*
    by V. Khlebnikov and A. Kruchenykh.

26. *Portrait of M. V. Matiushin,* 1913.
    Oil on canvas,
    41⅞×41⅞ in. (106.3×106.3 cm).
    State Tretyakov Gallery, Moscow.

27. *Soldier of the First Division,* 1914.
    Oil and collage on canvas,
    21⅛×17⅝ in. (53.6×44.8 cm).
    The Museum of Modern Art, New York.

28. *Composition with Mona Lisa,* 1914.
    Oil and collage on canvas,
    24¼×19½ in. (62×49.5 cm).
    State Russian Museum, Leningrad.

29. *An Englishman in Moscow,* 1914.
    Oil on canvas,
    34⅝×22½ in. (88×57 cm).
    Stedelijk Museum, Amsterdam.

30. *The Aviator,* 1914.
    Oil on canvas,
    49¼×25⅝ in. (125×65 cm).
    State Tretyakov Gallery, Moscow.

31. *Black Square* [1913] 1923–29.
    Oil on canvas,
    41¾×41⅞ in. (106.2×106.5 cm).
    State Russian Museum, Leningrad.

32. *Black Circle* [1913] 1923–29.
    Oil on canvas,
    41½×41½ in. (105.5×105.5 cm).
    State Russian Museum, Leningrad.

33. *Black Cross* [1913] 1923–29.
    Oil on canvas,
    41⅞×41⅞ in. (106.4×106.4 cm).
    State Russian Museum, Leningrad.

34. *Red Square: Painterly Realism of a Peasant Woman in Two Dimensions,* 1915.
    Oil on canvas,
    20⅞×20⅞ in. (53×53 cm).
    State Russian Museum, Leningrad.

35. *Suprematism: Self-Portrait in Two Dimensions,* 1915.
    Oil on canvas,
    31½×24⅜ in. (80×62 cm).
    Stedelijk Museum, Amsterdam.

36. *Suprematist Painting: Aeroplane Flying,* 1915.
    Oil on canvas,
    22⅝×19 in. (57.3×48.3 cm).
    The Museum of Modern Art, New York.

37. *Suprematism,* 1915.
    Oil on canvas,
    34½×28⅜ in. (87.5×72 cm).
    State Russian Museum, Leningrad.

38. *Black Square and Red Square,* 1915.
    Oil on canvas,
    28×17½ in. (71.1×44.4 cm).
    The Museum of Modern Art, New York.

39. *Suprematist Composition,* 1915.
    Oil on canvas,
    27⅝×18½ in. (70×47 cm).
    Fine Arts Museum, Tula.

40. *Suprematism,* 1916–17.
    Oil on canvas,
    31½×31½ in. (80×80 cm).
    Fine Arts Museum, Krasnodar.

41. *Supremus No. 56,* 1916.
    Oil on canvas,
    31¾×28 in. (80.5×71 cm).
    State Russian Museum, Leningrad.

42. *Suprematism (Supremus No. 58),* 1916.
Oil on canvas,
31¼×27¾ in. (79.5×70.5 cm).
State Russian Museum, Leningrad.

43. *Suprematist Painting,* 1916.
Oil on canvas,
34⅝×27⅝ in. (88×70 cm).
Stedelijk Museum, Amsterdam.

44. *Suprematist Painting,* 1915–16.
Oil on canvas,
19¼×17⅜ in. (49×44 cm).
Wilhelm Hacke Museum, Ludwigshafen.

45. *Suprematist Painting,* 1917.
Oil on canvas,
38×25¾ in. (96.5×65.4 cm).
The Museum of Modern Art, New York.

46. *Suprematist Painting: Yellow Quadrilateral on White,* 1917–18.
Oil on canvas,
41¾×27¾ in. (106×70.5 cm).
Stedelijk Museum, Amsterdam.

47–54. Eight lithographs from *Suprematism: 34 Drawings,* 1920.
Vitebsk Unovis. (Actual size.)

55. *Suprematism: White on White,* 1918.
Oil on canvas,
31×31 in. (78.7×78.7 cm).
The Museum of Modern Art, New York.

56. *Suprematist Painting,* 1920–25.
Oil on canvas,
31¼×31¼ in. (79.3×79.3 cm).
The Museum of Modern Art, New York.

57. *Future Planits for Leningrad. The Pilot's House,* 1924.
Pencil on paper,
12×17¾ in. (30.5×45 cm).
Stedelijk Museum, Amsterdam.

58. *Future Planits for Earth Dwellers,* 1923–24.
Pencil on paper,
17⅜×12⅛ in. (44×30.8 cm).
Stedelijk Museum, Amsterdam.

59. *Modern Buildings,* 1922–24.
Pencil on paper,
14⅛×21⅛ in. (36×53.5 cm).
Stedelijk Museum, Amsterdam.

60. *Gota,* 1923?
Plaster,
33½×18⅞×22⅞ in. (85.2×48×58 cm).
Musée National d'Art Moderne, Paris.

61. *Zeta,* 1923–27.
Plaster,
31¼×22⅜×28⅛ in. (79.4×56.7×71.4 cm).
Musée National d'Art Moderne, Paris.

62. *Suprematist Ornaments,* 1927.
18 plaster elements, overall dimension at base,
17¾×23⅝ in. (45×60 cm).
Musée National d'Art Moderne, Paris.

63. *Beta,* before 1926.
Plaster,
10¾×23⅜×39⅛ in. (27.3×59.5×99.3 cm).
Musée National d'Art Moderne, Paris.

64. *Jobless Girl* [1904].
Oil on canvas,
31½×26 in. (80×66 cm).
State Russian Museum, Leningrad.

65. *Spring,* after 1927.
Oil on canvas,
20⅞×26 in. (53×66 cm).
State Russian Museum, Leningrad.

66. *Reapers,* after 1927.
Oil on wood,
28×40⅝ in. (71×103.2 cm).
State Russian Museum, Leningrad.

67. *Woman with a Yellow Hat* [1908].
Oil on canvas,
18⅞×15⅜ in. (48×39 cm).
State Russian Museum, Leningrad.

68. *Carpenter,* 1927.
Oil on plyboard,
28⅜×21¼ in. (72×54 cm).
State Russian Museum, Leningrad.

69. *At the Dacha,* after 1928.
Oil on wood,
42½×28⅜ in. (108×72 cm).
State Russian Museum, Leningrad.

70. *The Harvest,* after 1928.
Oil on wood,
28⅝×20¾ in. (72.8×52.8 cm).
State Russian Museum, Leningrad.

71. *Small Boy (Vanka),* after 1927.
Oil on canvas,
28⅜×20¼ in. (72×51.5 cm).
State Russian Museum, Leningrad.

72. *At the Harvest (Marfa and Vanka),* after 1927.
Oil on canvas,
32¼×24 in. (82×61 cm).
State Russian Museum, Leningrad.

73. *Reaper,* 1928–30.
Oil on canvas,
33¾×25⅞ in. (85.8×65.6 cm).
State Russian Museum, Leningrad.

74. *Head of a Peasant,* 1928–30?
Oil on plywood,
28¼×21⅛ in. (71.7×53.8 cm).
State Russian Museum, Leningrad.

75. *Peasant in the Fields,* 1928–30?
Oil on plywood,
28⅛×17⅜ in. (71.3×44.2 cm).
State Russian Museum, Leningrad.

76. *Girls in the Field,* 1928–30.
Oil on canvas,
41¾×49¼ in. (106×125 cm).
State Russian Museum, Leningrad.

77. *Complex Presentiment: Half-Figure in a Yellow Shirt,* 1928–32.
Oil on canvas,
39×31⅛ in. (99×79 cm).
State Russian Museum, Leningrad.

78. *Peasant Woman,* 1929–30?
Oil on canvas,
38¾×31½ in. (98.5×80 cm).
State Russian Museum, Leningrad.

79. *Two Peasants,* 1928–32.
Oil on canvas,
20⅞×27⅝ in. (53×70 cm).
State Russian Museum, Leningrad.

80. *Three Female Figures,* 1928–30.
Oil on canvas,
18½×25 in. (47×63.5 cm).
State Russian Museum, Leningrad.

81. *Sportsmen,* 1928–30.
Oil on canvas,
55⅞×64⅝ in. (142×164 cm).
State Russian Museum, Leningrad.

82. *Red Cavalry,* 1930–31.
Oil on canvas,
35⅞×55⅛ in. (91×140 cm).
State Russian Museum, Leningrad.

83. *Landscape with a White House,* c. 1930.
Oil on canvas,
23¼×23½ in. (59×59.6 cm).
State Russian Museum, Leningrad.

84. *Landscape with Five Houses,* c. 1932.
Oil on canvas,
32⅝×24⅜ in. (83×62 cm).
State Russian Museum, Leningrad.

85. *Red House,* 1932.
Oil on canvas,
24¾×21⅝ in. (63×55 cm).
State Russian Museum, Leningrad.

86. *Torso: Half-Figure with a Pink Face,* 1928–32.
Oil on canvas,
28⅜×25⅝ in. (72×65 cm).
State Russian Museum, Leningrad.

87. *Half-Figure (Prototype of a New Image),* 1928–32.
Oil on canvas,
18⅛×14⅝ in. (46×37 cm).
State Russian Museum, Leningrad.

88. *Female Portrait,* 1928–32.
Oil on plywood,
22⅞×19¼ in. (58×49 cm).
State Russian Museum, Leningrad.

89. *Three Women,* 1928–32.
Oil on wood,
22½×18⅞ in. (57×48 cm).
State Russian Museum, Leningrad.

90. *Female Half-Figure,* 1928–32.
Oil on wood.
State Russian Museum, Leningrad.

91. *Two Male Figures,* 1930–32.
Oil on canvas,
39×29⅛ in. (99×74 cm).
State Russian Museum, Leningrad.

92. *Peasant,* 1928–32.
Oil on canvas,
47¼×39⅜ in. (120×100 cm).
State Russian Museum, Leningrad.

93. *Bathers,* 1928–32.
Oil on canvas,
38¾×31⅛ in. (98.5×79 cm).
State Russian Museum, Leningrad.

94. *Five Figures with Hammer and Sickle,*
c. 1930–32.
Pen and ink on paper,
3×4¾ in. (7.6×12 cm).
Musée National d'Art Moderne, Paris.

95. *The Arrest. Man and Power,* after 1930.
Pencil on paper,
13×8½ in. (33×21.7 cm).
Private collection.

96. *Running Man,* 1932–34.
Oil on canvas,
31⅛×25⅝ in. (79×65 cm).
Musée National d'Art Moderne, Paris.

97. *Head of a Young Girl of Today,* 1932.
Oil on canvas,
17⅛×13⅜ in. (43.5×34 cm).
State Russian Museum, Leningrad.

98. *Girl with Comb in Hair,* 1932–33.
Oil on canvas,
14×12¼ in. (35.5×31 cm).
State Tretyakov Gallery, Moscow.

99. *Girl with Red Pole,* 1932–33.
Oil on canvas,
28×24 in. (71×61 cm).
State Tretyakov Gallery, Moscow.

100. *Male Portrait (N. Punin?),* 1933.
Oil on canvas,
28×22½ in. (71×57 cm).
State Russian Museum, Leningrad.

101. *Portrait of the Artist's Wife,* 1933.
Oil on canvas,
26⅝×22 in. (67.5×56 cm).
State Russian Museum, Leningrad.

102. *Portrait of Una,* c. 1932.
Oil on canvas,
20½×16¾ in. (52×42.4 cm).
Moderna Museet, Stockholm.

103. *Female Worker,* 1933.
Oil on canvas,
28×23½ in. (71.2×59.8 cm).
State Russian Museum, Leningrad.

104. *Portrait of the Artist's Daughter,* 1933–34.
Oil on canvas,
33½×24⅜ in. (85×61.8 cm).
State Russian Museum, Leningrad.

105. *Portrait of the Artist's Wife,* 1934.
Oil on canvas,
39⅛×29¼ in. (99.5×74.3 cm).
State Russian Museum, Leningrad.

106. *Self-Portrait,* 1933.
Oil on canvas,
28¾×26 in. (73×66 cm).
State Russian Museum, Leningrad.